The Winning Edge

The Student-Athlete's Guide to College Sports

Fifth Edition

Frances and James Killpatrick

Acknowledgements

We would like to thank all the athletic directors, sports information directors and their staffs, high school guidance counselors and coaches, college admissions people, student-athletes and their parents who shared their valuable information and experience with us. Without them, this book could not have been written. Our special thanks go to the leading coaches who provided their constructive insights into taking your sport to college.

For their guidance and support, we are particularly indebted to: Catharine Alexander, Sandra Brent, Alexander Carlyle, Charles Cavagnaro, Benjamin and Robert Clark, Bill Dobson, Stewart Faught, Anna Griswold, Cecil Hart, Jeff, Anne and Jordan Irving, Bill Kilpatrick, Randy Lambert, Scott Lindley, Dan Meier, Mike Mullan, Tish Oliver, John F. Oliver, Ruth Perlstein, Kitty Porterfield, Marcia Saneholtz, Karen Bizier Smith and The Rev. Robert Sunderland, S.J.

And last, but definitely not least, thanks to our grown children, Amy and Patrick, whose perceptive reading of the manuscript helped keep us in line.

© 1997 by Frances and James Killpatrick

All rights reserved.

Cover design by Bremmer & Goris
Typesetting by Edington-Rand Inc.

Address Correspondence to:

Octameron Associates, Inc.
P.O. Box 2748
Alexandria, VA 22301
(703) 836-5480
www.octameron.com

Address bookstore inquiries regarding purchases and returns to:
Dearborn Trade
155 North Wacker Drive
Chicago, IL 60606

Outside Illinois, 800/245-BOOK
In Illinois, 312/836-4400 x270

ISBN 1-57509-028-7
PRINTED IN THE UNITED STATES OF AMERICA

Contents

Section I

Taking Your Sport to College

It's the last game of your senior year in high school. Time to put away your sports equipment and all the memories that go with it and get on with life? No way!

College life and college sports are intertwined. And that doesn't mean just for the star football or basketball player for whom college may be a step on the road to a professional sports career.

College sports is a wide, wide world, encompassing everything from "factories" with facilities that make the pros jealous to intramural activities at a small college where the only requirement is the energy to get out on the field.

And that is what this book is all about. Helping you – the STUDENT-athlete (the emphasis is intentional) – sort through all the confusion and make a correct decision about where and how you will take your sport (or sports) to college. When this book first came out 10 years ago, the "typical" student we reached probably was a male. But that definitely is not true today. The veritable explosion of women's sports in high schools and the impact of federal Title IX legislation on the colleges (see Chapter 2) has changed the playing field. Today, our "typical" reader is just as likely to be a young woman.

This book is not aimed at the blue-chipper whose postal carrier has been groaning under the weight of mail from college coaches and whose phone has been ringing off the hook. He or she, might, however, do well to read the "rules" chapter to avoid violations that can derail even the most gifted (well-intentioned) athletes.

Our goal is to make the path a bit smoother for the better-than-average high school athlete who wants to keep competing while pursuing his or her college degree. To that end, we will tell you how scholarships and partial scholarships are awarded; how to match your athletic and academic skills with the right college; and how to use your sports to give you a winning edge in admission to those tough-to-get-into small colleges with strong sports traditions.

Along the way, we will explore the roles of other important players – your parents, your high school coaches, and your guidance counselors. We will tell you how to attract the notice of college coaches and how best to follow through once you have their interest.

To make your search for a college scholarship a little easier, we have included charts with the addresses and athletic department phone numbers for the 902 schools in the three divisions of the National Collegiate Athletic Association (NCAA) and also the 363 mostly smaller colleges in the National Association of Intercollegiate Athletics (NAIA). For NCAA Division I schools, we also include the latest graduation rate information.

Along with this you will find words of advice from some of America's most successful college coaches – from Penn State's Joe Paterno, whose football team is perennially one of the nation's best; to Sharon Goldbrenner-Pfluger of the College of New Jersey, whose teams have won six Division III field hockey championships and eight women's lacrosse crowns; to Jim Steen, the swimming coach at Kenyon College, whose men's teams have won 18 consecutive Division III championships and whose women's teams have won 14 in a row.

Tighter Academic Standards ... Improved Graduation Rates

Let's go back to the subject of graduation rates. In many ways, the issue epitomizes a period in which there have been nearly as many headlines about the problems and scandals of college sports as about what the teams did on the playing field. True, there are more than enough scandals to go around, but they do not typify the bulk of college sports.

The latest report showed, for example, that a larger percentage of students who received athletics-related aid at NCAA Division I schools graduated within six years than did the student bodies as a whole. For all students, 56 percent of those who entered in the fall of 1990 graduated by August 1996. Among those with athletic scholarships, 58 percent graduated in that same six-year period.

The annual surveys, which began shortly after Proposition 48 imposed tighter academic standards for eligibilities, have shown a consistent increase in the graduation rate for student-athletes – in large part because of the outstanding records posted by female athletes, both white and black. In the most recent figures, 68 percent of all female student-athletes graduated within six years compared with a 58 percent graduation rate for all female students. The graduation rate for black female student-athletes was 59 percent, well above the 42 percent mark for all black female students.

On the other side of the gender coin, 53 percent of male student-athletes graduated within six years, slightly below the 54 percent rate for all male students. The rate for black male student-athletes was 43 percent, 10 percentage points better than the average for all black male students.

Male basketball players continue to drag down the averages. The average for those entering in 1990 was just 45 percent – but still a 3 percentage point gain from two years earlier. The rate for white male basketball players was 58 percent and the rate for black male basketball players was 39 percent, 2 percentage points better than those who enrolled in 1988. By comparison, the graduation rate for football players entering as freshmen in 1990 was 52 percent, 4 percentage points down from the 1988 freshmen.

Cleaning Up College Sports

The negative image that has plagued college sports in recent years goes beyond graduation rates, however. Several years ago, the Knight Foundation Commission on Intercollegiate Athletics came up with a wide-ranging list of recommendations to increase academic performance, impose tighter financial rules (including the outside income of coaches) and put the major responsibility for cleaning up sports on college presidents and trustees.

The message is being heard. College and university presidents have assumed a tougher role within the NCAA. There have been cuts in the number of coaches and in the number of scholarships awarded (including for football and basketball). In addition, new restrictions on practice time, length of seasons and use of athletic dormitories have been imposed. And these changes come on top of the continually toughening Proposition 48 standards. In 1993, the NCAA approved an athletics certification plan that requires schools to conduct a self-study of their sports programs (with outside peer review) at least once every five years to verify that the programs are meeting the desired goals. These include:

- An athletic program designed to be "a vital part of the institution's educational system."
- A policy of admitting only student-athletes who have reasonable expectations of obtaining degrees. Schools will be asked to explain if there is a significant difference between the graduation rate of athletes and the student body as a whole, and if the academic profile of entering student-athletes differs from that of the rest of the student body.
- Adequate academic support services for athletes.
- A schedule of practice and games that minimizes "conflicts between athletics participation and academic schedules, especially during examination periods."

Some college officials see the certification process as a way to level the playing fields between schools that sincerely are trying to comply with both the letter and spirit of the rules and those that aren't. Similar sentiments are becoming evident in the student ranks, as well as with students realizing that college sports are more than a farm system for the pros. A survey of major college football players found that 89 percent said they were attending college to gain an education while just 8 percent said their aim was to prepare for a pro career.

For all the evidence that the NCAA has turned the corner, the road still has many bumps ahead.

"There's no doubt we are moving in the right direction," said Charles Cavagnaro, the now-retired University of Memphis athletic director, who was hired in the wake of a scandal over the low graduation rate of its basketball players, "but we still have a way to go."

Ultimately, the headlines have little too do with the average college student-athlete. Consider that 322,763 students – 123,207 women and 199,556 men – participated in intercollegiate athletics at NCAA schools in 1995-96 and compare that to the number of sports scandals. There is ample room for you – the typical STUDENT-athlete – to make college sports an important and pleasurable part of your higher education.

And now back to that final contest – and we sincerely hope you started thinking about your athletic future long before the end of your senior year. This is a complicated process with many options for both student and college. To compete successfully, you need an early start and plenty of support. That's exactly what this book provides.

The Wide, Wide World of Financial Aid

Financial aid and college athletics are like teammates. Quite simply, you may be able to use your athletic abilities to help pay the cost of your college education.

Note that we said "help pay." While technically the "four-year free ride" is still out there (mainly in football and basketball), unless coaches are already camping on your doorstep, don't count on it.

As a good to excellent athlete, a more realistic goal should be to see how large an athletic scholarship may be available – or to what extent your sports abilities will help you get into a school where you can qualify for financial assistance based on your individual needs.

Classifying the Colleges

First, let's take a look at how colleges and universities are classified, since this classification governs the aid they can give their student- athletes.

NCAA Division I

These schools are the "biggies," especially those with Division I-A football programs (In the football only, Division I gets divided into Division I-A and Divisions I-AA). This group consists of the major state universities and the independent sports powers you see on television. Guidelines require these schools to compete "at the highest feasible level" in either football or basketball, with the program being regional or national in scope. These schools compete primarily with other Division I schools.

Division I schools must offer at least seven varsity sports for men's or mixed teams and seven for women's teams, with schools being given the option of having six sports for men's or mixed teams and eight for women'. Indoor and outdoor track can be counted as two sports.

Schools with Division I-A football teams also must have stadiums that seat at least 30,000, average 17,000 paid attendance at home games and play more than 60 percent of their football games against other Division I-A teams. In most cases, Division I-A teams are the ones you see in the big year-end bowl games. Since there is no Division I-A playoff, the "champion" is selected by the Associated Press poll of sportswriters and the *USA Today* poll of coaches. There is growing pressure, however, to set up a playoff system that would lead up to a lucrative college "superbowl."

Schools with Division I-AA football programs must play more than half their football games against Division I-A or I-AA teams. In Division I-AA, teams do have a playoff to determine the national championship.

In every other sport, the NCAA treats all Division I schools the same, specifying a minimum number of games or matches for each sport. For example, in basketball, both men's and women's teams may not play more than four games a year against opponents who are not in Division I.

Although Division I schools have a reputation for conducting enormous sports operations, the NCAA places strict limits on how many scholarships the schools may actually award. And a few Division I schools, notably in the Ivy League, offer only need-based financial aid. As a general rule, Division I schools maintain very competitive programs and actively recruit athletes.

Recent rules changes have been aimed at schools that were in Division I mainly for basketball, while playing football at the Division II or III level. These rule changes include increasing the required number of varsity sports and the amount of financial aid (it must be at least $316,500 − adjusted annually for inflation − for both men's and women's sports, exclusive of football and basketball). Effective in the 1993-94 school year, these schools also had to switch their football programs to Division I or drop the sport altogether. A number have adopted what one official called "cost-containment football" − a Division I-AA schedule, but with need-based financial aid only and a limit on the number of coaches and the size of traveling squads..

NCAA Division II

This division is just a step behind Division I in size of programs. It includes many smaller state-supported schools − but can be nearly as competitive in terms of seeking out athletes. The number of scholarships permitted is much lower than the Division I limit in football, but only slightly behind in most other sports.

Division II schools must offer four varsity sports for men or mixed teams and four for women. More than half of football and basketball games must be against Division I or Division II schools. The minimum number of contests required is lower than for Division I. There are national playoffs in football as well as in other sports.

NCAA Division III

No athletic scholarships are permitted in this division. Financial aid is awarded solely on the basis of financial need. Student-athletes cannot be treated more favorably than other students. This group includes most of the prestigious small colleges with highly competitive admissions. Many Division III schools have proud athletic rivalries and traditions, however, and your sports abilities can help you get in the door and receive an aid package with more grants than loans.

Division III schools must sponsor four varsity sports for men or mixed teams and four for women. The minimum number of contests is lower still than Division II. More than half of football and basketball games must be against other Division III colleges.

NAIA

Any four-year college is eligible for membership in the National Association of Intercollegiate Athletics, but its more than 350 schools tend to be smaller ones.

The NAIA is organized by districts. There are post-season district tournaments in some sports as well as national championships. There are two levels of competition in football and basketball, but otherwise all schools compete for the same titles. Many NAIA schools have excellent sports programs, and most offer some athletic scholarships. A small number of schools belong to both the NAIA and some division of the NCAA.

Other Classifications

Other organizations include the National Christian College Athletic Association (NCCAA), the National Bible College Athletic Association (NBCAA) and National Little College Athletic Association (NLCAA). Member schools are often small church-affiliated colleges. They may or may not offer athletic scholarships. Many also belong to either the NAIA or the NCAA.

Exceptions to the Rule

How do you know which schools belong to what national organization and division? The tables in this book will help you. But remember, there are a few exceptions that may be important in helping you assess a college's sports program. An NCAA school is allowed to compete in a higher division in one men's and one women's sport (except for football and basketball). In general, this happens when a school has a very competitive program in that sport. For example, Division III Johns Hopkins plays Division I men's lacrosse. Similarly, a school can play a lower division schedule in one sport (except football), if it meets all the NCAA requirements (no athletic scholarships in a Division III sport, for example).

Grants-in-Aid: How Much and How Many

Athletic scholarships, or grants-in-aid as the colleges call them, are generally limited by both the NCAA and the NAIA to tuition and fees, room and board and the cost of required course-related books. The exception is NCAA Division III schools where need alone, not athletic ability, determines the amount of financial help. But even in Division III, the total package cannot exceed the official cost of attending that school – each college sets its own figure, one that includes transportation and incidental expenses in addition to the standard tuition, fees, books and room and board.

In instances where the student receives only a partial grant-in-aid, the NCAA allows Division I and II colleges to provide some need-based assistance above that athletic scholarship, so long as the total does not exceed the value of a full grant-in-aid (which, again, is limited to tuition, fees, required books, room and board). Money earned under a college's work-study program is included in this equation but student loans are not. There is a partial exception for Pell Grants from the federal government. But the total aid package, including the Pell Grant, cannot exceed the value of a full grant-in-aid by more than $2,400 a year in Division I ($1,500 a year in Division II) or the average cost of attendance for that school, whichever is less.

In a recent development, Division I athletes are now permitted to hold part-time jobs, earning up to the difference between the aid they are receiving and the school's cost of attendance. It is up to the colleges to police these jobs, making sure that student athletes are not getting some sort of special "deal" because of their sports status.

In figuring the total aid package, your family's ability to contribute is a factor mainly in Division III schools, where all financial aid must be based on need and provided without consideration for athletic participation.

Need-based aid doesn't sound as glamorous as an athletic scholarship, but many Division III coaches point out that the total assistance over a four-year period may well be greater than you would get with a partial scholarship at a non-Division III school. The real test is how much you and your parents spend for college, out of your own pocket.

Gender Equity: Slowly But Surely

"No person in the United States shall, on the basis of sex, be excluded from participation in, be denied the benefits of, or be subjected to discrimination under any education program or activity receiving federal financial assistance."

That's the text of Title IX of the Education Act of 1972. Bringing meaning to the words is the hottest topic in college sports today. Although the law has been in effect for more than 25 years, its implementation received a major boost in the spring of 1997 when the Supreme Court refused to hear a challenge from Brown University. Any school that receives federal money – which means virtually every school in the country – must now move promptly to get on the right side of Title IX. Within weeks after the high court ruling, the National Women's Law Center filed Title IX complaints against 25 colleges and universities. More suits are sure to follow.

Title IX Crash Course

In 1979, the Education Department's Office of Civil Rights established a three-prong test to determine whether college athletic programs satisfied Title IX.

* The percentage of men and women on varsity team rosters must "substantially" match the percentage of men and women in the school's full-time, undergraduate student body.

If a school cannot meet this proportionality standard, it is in violation of the law unless it can show:

* It has a recent history of adding sports for the underrepresented gender (almost always women); or
* It can prove it is accommodating the interests and abilities of its all students (Brown failed this part of the test when it tried to drop two men's sports and two women's sports).

Schools also can be challenged in two other areas under Title IX:

* If the percentage of scholarship money given to men and women doesn't reflect the percentage of men and women in the varsity sports programs;

If all other aspects of the sports programs – such as equipment, practice times, coaching, publicity and travel schedules – are not equivalent.

Although the number of women competing in college sports is climbing steadily, a study released by the NCAA found that women made up 53 percent of the enrollment of Division I schools but only 37 percent of the varsity athletes. Colleges are thus dealing with the Title IX challenges in a number of ways: adding new varsity sports for women, dropping men's sports programs (wrestling, gymnastics and swimming have been hit the hardest), and limiting the number of non-scholarship athletes on team rosters to help even out the numbers game. Football remains a major sticking point. There is no women's sport that can match up with the number of scholarships (85 full ones in Division I-A) and team members. But big-time football programs help pay the freight for other sports and athletic directors are reluctant to change things. Many observers think there will have to be major changes in the NCAA rules if full compliance with Title IX is to be achieved. Donna Lopiano, the former Texas women's athletic director who now heads the Women's Sports Foundation, questions, for example, whether third- and fourth-stringers in football really need full scholarships, or could they get along on partial ones like athletes in other sports.

One sport that has blossomed in the search for Title IX compliance is women's rowing. So many schools have upgraded it from a club sport to full varsity status that the NCAA held a national championship regatta for the first time in the spring of 1997. Not only does rowing offer the equivalent of 20 full scholarships for women, but it can accommodate a larger roster of athletes than most other women's sports. Also, rowing relies more heavily on conditioning and strength than on the skills required by some other sports, making it attractive even to women who may not have had a chance to row in high school.

Why is it so important that women get a fair shake in college sports? It goes beyond fun and games. Women who play sports are generally more successful than women who don't. They have higher high school (and college) graduation rates, lower teenage pregnancy rates, and a better chance of avoiding abusive relationships. The Title IX controversy makes it more important for young women to consider making college sports a part of their future plans.

The Women's Sports Foundation, a nonprofit educational organization begun in 1974 by tennis great Billie Jean King, provides information services, publishes a list of women's intercollegiate athletic scholarships and actively advocates equal opportunities for women in sports (for details, call 1-800-227-3988).

Counting the Players

The numbers and types of athletic scholarships available for both men and women vary widely with the sport and the school's classification. The formulas can get complicated, with an actual head count imposed in a few sports, while in others, the limit is an equivalent number of full scholarships. This allows coaches to split up their scholarship dollars among many more athletes. For example, one award might be divided between five athletes with one receiving a half-scholarship, and four others receiving eighth-scholarships. Here, in simplified form, are the limits:

NCAA Division I

In football, Division I-A institutions can have a total of 85 football players on scholarship at any one time, with no more than 25 grants awarded in any year. Division I-AA schools are limited to the equivalent of 63 full grants-in-aid in football, with no more than 30 awarded in any year.

Division I men's basketball programs had the number of scholarships cut from 15 to 13 in 1993, but the limit on scholarships for women's basketball remains at 15.

Both Division I-A football and men's and women's Division I basketball have full scholarships only, with no splitting of grants permitted.

Other Division I sports with a limit on the total number of athletes on scholarship are: women's gymnastics, 12; women's tennis, 8; women's volleyball, 12.

Men's sports with a limit based on an equivalent number of scholarships are (after a 10 percent cutback in 1993): baseball, 11.7; cross country/track, 12.6; fencing, 4.5; golf, 4.5; gymnastics, 6.3; ice hockey, 18; lacrosse, 12.6; rifle, 3.6; skiing, 6.3; soccer, 9.9; swimming, 9.9; tennis, 4.5; volleyball, 4.5; water polo, 4.5; and wrestling, 9.9.

Women's sports and their equivalency levels are: archery, 5; badminton, 6; bowling, 5; crew, 20; cross country/track, 18; fencing, 5; field hockey, 12; golf, 6; ice hockey, 18; lacrosse, 12; skiing, 7; soccer, 12; softball, 12; squash, 12; swimming, 14; synchronized swimming, 5; team handball, 10; and water polo, 8.

NCAA Division II

All sports are subject to an equivalency test rather than a head count. Football squads, for example, are limited to the equivalent of 36 scholarships in any academic year.

Other scholarship maximums:

Men's sports: baseball, 9; basketball, 10; cross country/track, 12.6; fencing, 4.5; golf, 3.6; gymnastics, 5.4; ice hockey, 13.5; lacrosse, 10.8; rifle, 3.6; skiing, 6.3; soccer, 9; swimming, 8.1; tennis, 4.5; volleyball, 4.5; water polo, 4.5; and wrestling, 9.

There is an additional limitation for men in Division II. No school can provide more than 60 scholarships (or the equivalent) in sports other than football and basketball in any academic year.

Women's sports: archery, 5; badminton, 8; basketball, 10; bowling, 5; crew, 20; cross country/track, 12.6; fencing, 4.5; field hockey, 6.3; golf, 5.4; gymnastics, 6; ice hockey, 18; lacrosse, 9.9; skiing, 6.3; soccer, 9.9; softball, 7.2; squash, 9; swimming, 8.1; synchronized swimming, 5; team handball, 12; tennis, 6; volleyball, 8; and water polo, 8.

NCAA Division III

Since aid is unrelated to athletics, there is no limit on how many student-athletes can receive need-based financial assistance.

NAIA

There are no limits on the number of awards per sport, but because many NAIA schools have small budgets, the number of scholarships is often limited by the cash available.

Partial Scholarships

A close look at the limits on sports scholarships, other than those in "revenue sports" of football and basketball that keep college athletic programs solvent, makes it easy to understand why partial scholarships have become so important. A swimming coach in Division I could not begin to fill his lanes if he gave his 9.9 scholarships to 10 male athletes (or his 14 scholarships for women to 14 females). And it's even harder in Division II with a limit of 8.1 apiece for men and women. But if the coach fragments those scholarships – room and board to a diver, tuition for a freestyler, books to a backstroker, etc. – he can put more bodies into the pool and field a more competitive team.

When Wichita State won the College World Series in 1989, not one member of the team was on a full scholarship. Coach Gene Stephenson had split his 13 full grants-in-aid (the limit has since dropped to 11.7) 27 different ways. Although he says he thinks all of his players deserved a full scholarship, he was doing the most he could with the resources at hand.

This scenario repeats itself season after season in most of the "non-revenue" sports – those that bring in less money at the gate than it costs to field a team. Prospective students must work out the best arrangements they can.

It should be noted that the above lists show the maximum number of scholarships allowed per sport; a college does not have to fund them all. In fact, Division I schools are required to meet just one of several minimum tests:

• Award at least half of the possible grants in each sport.
• Spend at least $316,500 on men's sports, exclusive of football and basketball, and 316,500 on women's sports, exclusive of basketball, with the figure adjusted for inflation annually.
• Award the equivalent of 19 full grants-in-aid for women and 19 for men, exclusive of football and men's and women's basketball.

Although NAIA coaches face no limits in numbers, partial scholarships are often used to help stretch the budget to cover more student-athletes.

Out-of-State Tuition Waivers

Another way for colleges, especially state-supported ones, to provide aid is to waive the extra tuition charged out-of-state students. This can amount to several thousand dollars, depending on the school. Some colleges may prefer to couple a tuition waiver with a partial scholarship. Ask about this when conferring with any college or university.

How Long, How Long

When we mentioned earlier that the "four-year free ride" was a thing of the past, we were referring not only to limits on the number of grants-in-aid, but also the length of the commitment.

Basic grants-in-aid can last for up to five years, but the aid is provided just one year at a time. Prospective athletes can be told, under NCAA rules, that the athletic department will recommend renewal of the aid for each of four years. Prospective applicants can even be told that such recommendations have always been followed in the past. The renewal is not automatic, however, and prospects have to know this.

The same rules apply to continued aid to a student-athlete who is injured in competition. The athletic department can inform prospects about the school's usual policy in renewing aid to athletes who are injured or become ill. Again, renewal is not automatic for injured athletes, and prospects cannot be told it is.

An appeals process within the school is available to student-athletes whose financial aid is either reduced or canceled.

Need-based aid also is awarded on a year-to-year basis. The student must remain in good academic standing. His or her finances must be reviewed to determine whether there has been a major change in the family's ability to contribute toward education costs. In other words, if your parents hit the lottery or, conversely, the family farm goes under, the school wants to know! These are all points to clarify when you get around to talking to colleges or universities you may attend.

A World of Differences

Not all colleges are created equal: even the big-name sports schools vary widely in the levels of financial aid they offer their athletes. The major state universities, for example, can usually be counted on to provide close to the maximum amount of aid permitted by NCAA rules. But the Ivy League – Yale, Harvard, Princeton, Pennsylvania, et al – offers only need-based aid even though it plays a Division I schedule.

Then there are the hybrids. For example, Division I basketball powerhouse Georgetown University played a Division III schedule in football until 1993 and offers no athletic scholarships in football or several of its minor sports. On the other hand, Johns Hopkins University is a Division III school – except in men's lacrosse where it plays a Division I schedule, awards scholarships and regularly challenges for the national title.

In checking out a college or university, you need to find out exactly how many scholarships it offers in your sport and how those scholarships are likely to be divided.

The Rules of the Games

O ver the past few years, the official National Collegiate Athletic Association policy manual has tripled in size. Whereas it used to weigh about the same as a fair-sized city's telephone book, now it's like a large city's white and yellow pages combined. Its hundreds of pages might well have been written by a team of corporate lawyers. The rules are extremely complicated and can be confusing. But they are the rules – and they apply to you just as surely as they do to the 40-point-a-game scorer being courted by every Division I school in the country.

It is your responsibility to learn and follow the rules. The consequences of breaking them can be disastrous both to the student-athlete and the college or university. The NCAA may declare the student ineligible. It may bar the school from post-season play and/or television appearances, put the school on probation, or take away the school's scholarships. In the most flagrant cases, the NCAA may even impose the "death sentence" of barring a school from intercollegiate competition for a season or more.

The NCAA enforces its rules more strictly every year. You've seen the stories in the newspaper and on television: big-name schools called on the carpet for everything from charges of sending cash to a player's parents to driving an ineligible player to class. Pro sports agents have been tried for signing and paying players while they still played college sports.

To help you stay away from trouble, the NCAA publishes a handy "Guide for the College-Bound Student-Athlete." It is sold in bulk (50 copies for $12 from the NCAA, 6201 College Blvd., Overland Park, KS. 66211-2422). Your guidance department should have some. Get a copy. It's a good reference for you and your parents. The National Association of Intercollegiate Athletics has a similar "Guide for the College Bound Student." It is also available in bulk (50 copies for $15); single copies are free from the NAIA, 2 Warren Place, 1450 South Yale, Suite 1450, Tulsa, Okla. 74136-4223.

There also are a number of sports information sites on the Internet, if you're one who spends time surfing. The NCAA for example, can be reached at *http://www.ncaa.org* (you'll find the entire "Guide for the College-Bound Student-Athlete" on-line).

Here are some of the basic directives to help keep you on the right side of the rules.

The Recruiter Wants You

The recruiting of college student-athletes is a highly complicated – and tightly regulated – operation. As an average-to-good athlete, your challenge is probably going to be to catch the eye of college coaches or recruiters, not fend them off. Still, you need to know the rules so you can avoid costly missteps in this sensitive area.

NCAA Recruiting Rules—The Highlights

1. You become a "prospective student-athlete" (PSA) when you enter the ninth grade – earlier if a college or university provides you (or your relatives or friends) any financial aid or other benefits that it does not generally provide to prospective students.

2. You become a "recruited prospective student-athlete" at a college if a coach or other "representative" of the college's athletic interests (booster or representative) solicits you or any member of your family for the purpose of securing your enrollment and participation in intercollegiate athletics at that college.

   • Actions that make you a recruited prospective student-athlete include providing you transportation to the campus, entertaining you or any member of your family in any way on the campus (an exception is a free ticket to an athletic event when you visit with a group, such as your high school team), placing telephone calls to you or any member of your family, or visiting you or any member of your family anywhere other than the college campus.

   • A "representative of an institution's athletic interests" is anyone the college has asked to help recruit a student or anyone the school knows is trying to recruit for them. This includes boosters, alumni and such. Representatives are governed by the same rules as staff members, and schools are responsible for their actions. They are barred from recruiting in Division I, and their activities are limited in Division II. This limitation does not apply to alumni or representatives if the contact is part of the college's regular admissions program for all prospective students, including non-athletes.

3. A college coach can contact you in person off the college campus only on or after July 1 following your junior year in high school. Phone calls from coaches or faculty members also are barred before July 1 following your junior year in all sports except football (where the date is Aug. 15), and coaches may not accept collect calls from you before that date. Division III coaches, alumni and boosters can contact you any time after you complete your junior year.

4. Make sure your correct year in school is shown on all programs, letters and information you or your coach or guidance counselor may be using. The NCAA News publishes lists of rules infractions and their outcomes. Misinformation about a student-athlete's year is often the cause of a rule infraction as coaches contact a student before the right time making that student ineligible. The NCAA provides an appeals process, but it is by no means always successful.

5. Unfortunately, you cannot count on coaches to know all these rules, and their ignorance can prove to be your loss. One college ceased recruitment of a prospect because a volunteer coach provided a car for a college student-athlete to transport the prospect during his official visit.

6. You can make one 48-hour expense-paid trip to a college, but not before classes have started in your senior year. The school can pay for transportation (tourist class only if flying), room and board (at on-campus facilities if available) and modest entertainment. (A college host can be given $20 a day to cover all costs of entertaining you. But beware, this can't go for T-shirts or other such mementos. T-shirts, sweatshirts and caps have gotten more than one college in trouble. One case involved a student-athlete simply swapping his college jersey for a prospect's shirt. Don't do or accept anything like that.)

7. The school also can entertain parents or legal guardians during that one trip. Care is the watchword here, too. One basketball prospect was dropped because during his official visit, he and his father were provided seating in a skybox during a home football game. Regular seats would have been fine; extra treatment, no.

8. Colleges may not provide the trip unless you have provided them, in advance, a score from an SAT, ACT or PSAT taken on a national test date under national testing conditions. In Division I, the prospective student athlete also must provide a copy of her or his academic transcript. This transcript must also be mailed (or faxed) so it arrives before the student. It cannot be brought with the student, or faxed during the visit. The published infraction lists include several cases where students were dropped as prospects because they arrived on campus with or before their test results.

9. Also in Division I, if your sport is one that has an early signing period for the National Letter of Intent, you may not make an official visit unless you furnish the school proof that you have scores of at least 820 on the SAT, or 82 on the PSAT, or a sum total of 68 on the ACT or PACT Plus, and that you have at least a 2.0 average in at least nine core courses (if you don't have these credentials, your visit cannot start until 24 hours after the early signing period ends).

10. To simplify matters, the NCAA has established an initial-eligibility clearinghouse – run by the American College Testing Program – to certify to colleges that students meet all the requirements. You will have to go through the clearinghouse to establish eligibility before entering school. Your high school guidance counselor will have an information packet and the forms you need. There is an $18 fee, but your counselor can approve a fee waiver if you have been granted one for the SAT or ACT. Your counselor can obtain registration materials, at no cost, by calling (319) 337-1492.

11. In all, you can make expense-paid visits to a total of five NCAA Division I and Division II schools. This applies even if you are being recruited in more than one sport. There is no limit on the number of Division III schools you may visit.

12. You can visit a campus as many times as you want at your own expense. You do not have to wait to make these trips until your senior year. During those visits, a Division I school can provide up to three complimentary tickets to a campus athletic event – but nothing else. Division II schools also can provide a meal at an on-campus facility.

13. Just three in-person recruiting contacts with a prospect or his or her family at any location off the campus are permitted in Divisions I and II. In Divi-

sions I and II the contact must be made by an athletic department staff member who has been authorized to recruit. No funds may be spent for entertaining the student or her or his family. Coaches may evaluate you by watching practices or games on four occasions. A tournament held on consecutive days counts as one evaluation. There is no limit on contacts in Division III.

14. The recruiting calendar includes specific periods in each sport for evaluations and contacts. There also are so-called quiet periods, when in-person recruiting contacts can be made only on the college campus, and dead periods, when coaches may not contact prospective recruits either on- or off-campus and when both official and unofficial trips to the school are barred. Coaches still can call or write prospects during these periods. Be sure you know what the various periods are for your sport or sports. These are complicated rules and innocent violations are common. Take the recent example of one unknowing prospect who stopped by a head coach's office on her own during a dead period. The college had to drop her.

15. A college staffer or representative can describe the school's grant-in-aid program and recommend a prospect for receiving such aid – but an award is not official until it comes from the school's financial aid office. Again, only the school's regular financial aid authority can actually award aid!

16. A school may ask a prospect to undergo a medical examination by the regular team physician during his or her official on-campus visit. But Division I schools may not conduct, either on campus or off, any kind of practice or workout in which the student demonstrates his athletic ability.

17. Division II schools can, with permission of your high school athletic director, hold a tryout before enrollment but after you have completed your high school eligibility. This may include tests to evaluate your strength, speed, agility and sports skills. It may include competition in some sports, but not in football, ice hockey, lacrosse, soccer or wrestling.

18. NAIA schools can hold on-campus tryouts if that is a general practice – such as having auditions for music majors.

19. Developmental clinics that are open to the general public and designed to develop fundamental skills are not considered tryouts.

20. There are strict limits on what the college can provide a prospective student-athlete in terms of brochures or other printed information. And watch out for things like T-shirts and caps. They are definite no-nos.

Dangling Propositions

Academic requirements for student-athletes have been toughened in recent years. Much of the furor over Proposition 48 has faded, but the rules, now referred to by the NCAA as Bylaw 14.3, are here to stay. A bit of history may be in order.

Proposition 48

This rule went into effect for the 1986-87 school year amid rising concern that schools were admitting athletes who were unable to meet college-level academic demands. It established a standard for high school grades and standardized test scores that athletes would have to meet before being eligible to play at Division I and II schools.

The rules were tightened a notch at the NCAA's 1989 convention when it decided that, effective in 1990-91, partial qualifiers (student-athletes who had graduated from high school with a 2.0 average but who did not meet all the requirements of Proposition 48/Bylaw 14.3) could not receive financial aid in their freshman year. Opposition was led by black basketball coaches (Remember Georgetown's John Thompson stalking off the court at the start of a televised game to dramatize his point?) who argued that the SAT and ACT were culturally biased and that minority athletes would be unfairly affected by the rule. The Black Coaches Association is continuing to protest both the use of standardized test scores, as well as the reduction in the number of basketball scholarships from 15 to 13.

In subsequent years, the scholarship rules have been relaxed a bit. Since 1996, partial qualifiers in Division I who meet a sliding standard of grades and test scores are eligible for athletic scholarships and can practice on-campus with a team during their freshman year. In Division II, athletic grants-in-aid for freshmen partial qualifiers already was permitted. In both Division I and II, prospective student-athletes who fail to meet the tests for qualifiers or partial qualifiers are eligible to receive need-based aid. At the same time, the standards have steadily been raised.

At present, to be eligible in Division I and II schools a student-athlete must:

1. Graduate from high school with a C (2.0) average in a "core curriculum" of at least 13 basic academic courses. These must include three years of English (four in Division I), two of mathematics, two of social science, two units of natural or physical science (including one laboratory course), two additional years of English, mathematics or natural or physical science, (one additional year in Division I) and two years of other courses that can be from the above areas or can include foreign language, computer science, philosophy or nondoctrinal (comparative) religion.

2. Post a minimum score on the Scholastic Aptitude Test (SAT) or the American College Test (ACT). In Division II, the minimum SAT score is 820 for the re-centered version of the test, which means all those taken after April 1, 1995. On the ACT, the minimum sum score is 68. In Division I, eligibility is now based on a sliding scale that links the standardized test score and high school grades. The closer your high school grade point average is to the minimum 2.0, the higher test score you will have to make– up to 1010 on the SAT or 86 on the ACT.

Whether you call it Bylaw 14.3 or Proposition 48, athletes who meet only these minimum academic indices will be recruited only if they have extraordinary athletic skills. The average student-athlete must do much better in the classroom to have a chance of going on to collegiate play. In more selective colleges, athletic skills may be a big help in running the admissions hurdles, but only if your grades and test scores put you on that school's playing field.

These rules do not presently apply to Division III colleges. Eligibility for financial aid, practice and competition in Division III are governed by institutional, conference and other NCAA rules.

The Qualifier Index

Core GPA	Minimum Required SAT	Minimum Required Sum ACT
2.500 and above	820	68
2.475	830	69
2.450	840-850	70
2.425	860	70
2.400	860	71
2.375	870	72
2.350	880	73
2.325	890	74
2.300	900	75
2.275	910	76
2.250	920	77
2.225	930	78
2.200	940	79
2.175	950	80
2.150	960	80
2.125	960	81
2.100	970	82
2.075	980	83
2.050	990	84
2.025	1000	85
2.000	1010	86

Partial Qualifier Index

Core GPA	SAT	Sum ACT
2.750 and above	720	59
2.725	730	59
2.700	730	60
2.675	740-750	61
2.650	760	62
2.625	770	63
2.600	780	64
2.575	790	65
2.550	800	66
2.525	810	67

NAIA Rules

NAIA rules are less complex. To be eligible for sports in your freshman year, you must meet two out of three criteria: Graduate in the top half of your high school class; have an overall 2.0 GPA; score 860 on the SAT or 18 on the ACT. Those who don't qualify must sit out of sports for a year.

There also are NAIA benchmarks for continued competition. A student-athlete must have 24 semester hours of credit to play a second season, 48 for a third season and 72 (including 48 in general education or her or his major) for a fourth. Students must also maintain a 2.0 GPA to compete in their third and fourth years or have junior class standing or higher.

We'll go into the challenge of matching your academic skills with the right college in a later chapter.

When Is a Professional Not a Professional?

Despite perceptions that some college athletic programs have become farm teams for professional sports, the NCAA has articulated a few strict conditions. You CANNOT be eligible for intercollegiate athletics in any sport if you have:

- Agreed to be represented generally, rather than in a specific sport, by an agent or organization that will market your athletic ability or reputation.
- After becoming a college student-athlete, accepted pay for or allow your name and picture to be used for advertising or promoting the sale of any commercial product or service.

You CANNOT be eligible in your particular sport if you have:

- Signed a professional contract, asked that your name be put on a pro draft list, actually played on a professional team, taken pay or accepted the promise of pay in any form.
- Agreed to be represented by an agent or other marketing organization.
- Tried out with a professional sports organization while enrolled in college. (This rule can be tricky. A college softball player was ruled ineligible because she used her sports skills in trying out for an extra's spot in the filming of "A League of Their Own," the movie about women baseball players.)

You CAN be eligible for competition in a sport other than the one for which you have been paid (for example, if you played minor league baseball, you can still play college basketball). You also still can be eligible if:

- Prior to enrolling in college you tried out for a professional sport, even if you received expenses for the tryout, or if, before enrolling, you were paid to give instruction in a particular sport.
- You received compensation authorized by the U.S. Olympic Committee for loss of employment while preparing for or participating in the Olympic Games.

A student-athlete who is under contract to or receiving pay from a professional team cannot receive financial aid. But he or she can become eligible for aid again by severing ties with the pro sport, even if still bound by an option clause in a contract. Starting professional competition again while still having college eligibility left, however, is considered a violation of ethical conduct rules and means a ban from all intercollegiate sports.

One recent change allows underclassmen to make themselves available for the National Basketball Association draft and then change their minds if they are unhappy with where they were selected. This can be done just once, and the student-athlete must not have signed with an agent.

Drug Policies and Procedures

NCAA regulations require you to sign a drug-testing consent form each academic year. Testing occurs randomly on a year-round basis in Division I football and track and field and is also conducted at NCAA championships in all sports and at certified post-season bowl games. If you test positive for any banned substance, including steroids, you will lose at least one season of eligibility. Many schools and conferences also have their own policies on drug use that may affect your participation in intercollegiate athletics. A recent U.S. Supreme Court decision permitting drug testing of elementary and high school athletes should be a further warning to any student-athlete that drugs will not be tolerated.

Other Pitfalls

You may be contacted by a scouting service during high school. You should be aware that the NCAA does not sanction or endorse any such service and specifically prohibits them from receiving compensation based on the amount of the college scholarships you may be awarded. If you have a question about whether the scouting service meets NCAA rules, check it out with the NCAA office.

After your high school eligibility is over, football and basketball prospects can participate in only two high school all-star games in each sport. After starting your senior year in high school, you cannot participate in a sports camp or clinic held by an NCAA college.

The NCAA guide also reminds student-athletes that they must sign a statement each academic year about eligibility, recruitment, financial aid and amateur status. And it warns: "Do not jeopardize your eligibility through involvement in violations of NCAA legislation. Knowingly furnishing the NCAA or your college false or misleading information about your involvement or knowledge of an NCAA rules violation will make you ineligible."

Another Basic — Appraising Sports Skills

N ow comes the difficult part for both parents and student-athletes. You know what colleges can offer in the way of athletic scholarships and other financial aid for student-athletes. You know enough about the rules of the NCAA and other organizations to avoid any pitfalls. But how do you match up your individual sports skills to the proper level – indeed the proper school – for college play?

Appraising Your Skills

College coaches agree that one of the toughest tasks facing the college-bound student-athlete is a realistic appraisal of talent. How good are you? Can you play on a Division I or II team? Would you really be better off at a Division III school or some other small college?

Obviously, you need a hand in this. Your high school coach is a key player. More than anyone else, she or he can point you in the right direction. Of course there is more to choosing a college than just checking the athletic program. Your guidance counselor will help you meet the academic requirements of the college. Your parents will have to be involved in decisions regarding cost, distance from home, etc.

Those relationships will be examined in other chapters, but for right now there is no escaping the bottom line. This is your life and your decision, and you must be the one to face reality.

The appraisal process is more difficult for some student-athletes than for others. For example, if college coaches and recruiters are already calling, then someone else has already appraised your skills and decided your abilities match their level of competition. Unfortunately, most high school students trying to catch the eye of a college coach don't have that free ride.

A side note here about recruiting: it comes in all shapes and forms. If you are a superstar, the sky's the limit as far as interest is concerned. If you're like most other student-athletes, it's more likely that you'll receive questionnaires from colleges that have heard of you. How does the word get out? The sports pages, contact with high school coaches, letters or calls from alumni, etc.

This questionnaire will ask whether you have any interest in the school and include a number of questions about your athletic and academic accomplishments. By all means, take advantage of these. Answer promptly and completely, working with your parents, coach and guidance counselor to do the best job you can. Questionnaires provide chances for you to introduce yourself to colleges. But be aware, a college may send out hundreds of these forms, and the interest may go no farther.

You probably won't hear from a college other than in this fashion before early in your senior season (remember, rules bar any off-campus contact by a Division I or Division II coach until July 1 after the end of your junior year. Coaches and faculty members cannot phone prospective student-athletes before that date either. In football, no calls are permitted before August 15). By then you should be well on your way to assessing your athletic prospects.

Skill appraisal always is easier for students from large schools in populous areas. If you are such a student, you will likely have been exposed to a highly competitive sports scene. You will have played with or against athletes who have gone on to college sports. Are you as good as they were? Better? Check on how they did at the college level. Did they pick a school where they were able to compete and make sports an enjoyable part of their college lives? Or did they select the wrong place and end up sitting on the bench or, worse, dropping out? The mistakes of others can be a great guide.

A student-athlete in a small town or rural area may not have the same advantage. High school competition can be spotty with few college-level athletes with whom to compare skills.

Realistic skill appraisals are also much easier in some sports than in others. A track and field athlete's times and distances, a golfer's scores, a swimmer's times, a skier's point profile, a rower's erg scores; all are hard facts that can be presented to a college coach.

But other athletic skills are more subjective. A football player can have great 40-yard speed but not be able to elude tacklers after fielding a punt, or carry the ball without fumbling. A basketball player may have a great vertical leap measurement, but can she rebound in heavy traffic?

Sports Camps

Sports camps, summer leagues, AAU swim teams and other such activities are a great place to attract attention. You need to be selective, however, especially where sports camps are concerned. And remember you cannot attend one of these camps once you start your senior year of high school.

If you have your eye on a particular school which conducts a camp in your sport, by all means sign up. One of the stars of Indiana University's championship soccer team first came to the coach's attention at camp when he was just 12 years old. But you must use good judgment.

Don't enroll in a famous coach's camp if your own good sense tells you his or her college is way out of your league. Also, beware of some camps that advertise a huge roster of professional stars. Check to see whether these celebrities actually work with campers or just drop by to sign a few autographs.

Many coaches will not pay much attention to you at a camp until the summer after your sophomore year. You simply won't have matured enough. The summer after your junior year is when the serious looking is done. Keep that in mind if you are thinking about a camp that is far from home or very expensive.

There's a new rule that impacts on basketball players hoping to catch the eye of a Division I coach. Such coaches now are permitted to attend only institutional camps – ones conducted by an NCAA college or a member of its staff – or noninstitutional camps that have been certified by the NCAA. Ask about this before you sign up for a basketball camp.

Tournaments

District, regional and state tournaments in sports such as golf or tennis offer you a real opportunity to be noticed. A college coach will appreciate good scores or high finishes in such competition. For example, a 76 in a tournament may tell a golf coach more about your potential than a 72 practice round on your home course with no pressure. If your goal is to attend a school in your home state, concentrate your tournament efforts there. But if your aim is broader, you may have to shoot for a larger stage on which to show what you can do.

Never, Never Use Steroids

Don't let the desire to play college sports lead you to do something stupid and dangerous. A frightening number of high school athletes have experimented with anabolic ("tissue-building") steroids and other performance-enhancing drugs. The quick gains in size and strength are enticing, but the long-term medical consequences should shock anyone out of the notion. Physically, steroids can cause heart problems and liver and kidney damage, possibly cancer. Mentally, steroid use results in increased anger and aggressiveness and often includes nightmares, hallucinations depression, and sometimes suicide.

Tragic stories are becoming all too common, as the health consequences of using steroids begin to kick in. The late Lyle Alzado, a pro football superstar who died of inoperable cancer that he blamed on steroid use, denied for years he was using any such substances. Shortly before his death, he told Sports Illustrated, "I lied. I'm sorry success meant so much to me. If you're on steroids, stop. I should have."

Testing programs are becoming prevalent, as the need for reform gains more support among sports authorities and athletes themselves, but concern for your own body, not a fear of being caught, should be the major consideration. Also, any college coach who would condone use of such substances is not someone with whom you want to associate.

Presenting Your Skills

It is up to you, to prepare a realistic analysis of your skills and put it in a format that will catch a college coach's eye. This should include physical facts – height, weight, speed, etc. – as well as a summary of personal and team accomplishments. Don't pad this with things you can't back up, but don't leave out any pertinent facts either. Try to give the coach an accurate feel for what you have accomplished in sports and what you hope to do at the college level.

To do this, build a sports resume, following the guidelines adults use to apply for jobs. Chapter 7 and Appendix A provide detailed information about preparing a sports resume.

If your real value to the team is not the points you score but the help you give teammates – both on and off the field, college coaches need to know that. Coaches realize they can't have a star in every slot, and besides, they need players whose spirit makes the team a good working unit.

If you have a sportsmanship award as evidence of your team spirit, list it on your resume. If not, mention this quality in your accompanying cover letter.

Parents and the Process

"Be responsible for who you are and what you do" is the advice to student-athletes from a staff member of the University of South Carolina Athletic Department.

You should keep these words in mind during the important process of finding the right place for your college education. Obviously the Gamecocks staffer has seen enough student-athletes and their parents to know that personal responsibility is a top priority.

The Ideal Situation for a Close-to-Perfect Process

First, your parents (and surely they are not skipping this chapter) realize the goal is to choose a college where you will get the finest education possible, plus make lifelong friendships and compile happy memories of the playing fields. If an athletic scholarship can help achieve that goal, so much the better.

Second, you accept the responsibility for giving it your best. In the words of St. Jerome, "No athlete is crowned save by the sweat of his own brow."

But the venerated saint probably didn't have a mother and father who had given up many hours driving him to practices since the day he first stepped up to the plate in a T-ball league.

You, in turn, recognize and appreciate the hopes and dreams your parents have for you. They cheered you on when you won and cheered you up when you lost, and they don't intend to stop now. Try to understand this, work together and remember this is the close-to-perfect situation. Many students reading this know the other side – parents who were just "too busy to get to the game," time after time after time.

In the ideal situation, you and your parents start serious planning in your sophomore year. No big pressure, just become acquainted with admissions rules, read up on colleges, get to know your high school coaches, teachers and your guidance counselors. Because you and your parents take the time to do this, you can plan your college visits with no last-minute rush, you can take all the right courses and pre-college academic tests, and you can get an accurate assessment of your athletic level of play. If you are a blue-chipper, your parents make it their business to learn all the high pressure recruiting techniques so they won't be carried away by guarantees of glory. (See Chapter 3.)

Now you are ready to apply to colleges. With the help of your high school coaches and guidance counselors, you have a realistic idea of whether and where you can get some kind of financial aid based on your athletic talent. Or you know where you can continue playing your sport as an enrichment of your college experience.

You send in applications on time (don't forget to make copies) and wait for acceptances. When they arrive, you and your parents consider all the options. You make the final decision, your parents tell you how proud they are, and everybody celebrates at your favorite restaurant.

A More Realistic Situation

That was the ideal. What's the reality?

Divorce isn't fatal, but statistics show that many of you won't be making these decisions with Mom and Dad sitting around the dining room table drinking hot chocolate. That's OK, too. Depending on your special situation, your parents can still go through all the research and give you the support you need. It's important to know that if relationships are not friendly, your coach and guidance counselor or a caring teacher, can provide help, information, a calm voice and support.

Here's another possible scenario. What about the Football Father who made it very clear his major goal in life is seeing Sonny follow in his footsteps at old State U? Fine, if that's what Sonny wants, too, and if he can make it through the admissions process. That may not be as easy as it was 25 years ago, and Dad needs to know that.

The opposite of this situation is the father or mother who was an unsuccessful athlete but wants to enjoy the thrill of victory through their talented children. This can be a delightful family experience, of course, when treated with joy and pride. But not with pressure.

Problems also arise when parents have unrealistic estimates of their children's talents. This can happen in large city high schools, but it's more likely to occur in a small town where an average young athlete becomes a star because the competition is less fierce. College coaches spend a lot of time dealing with parents whose child has been rejected for a scholarship or admission and who keep saying, "But she was the star of every game in high school."

This should start you and your family thinking. Let's go back to how parents can help.

Prepare Your Student to Leave Home

More than one university athletic administrator named good old-fashioned homesickness as one of the biggest problems many families don't face up to when choosing a college. The family is so excited over a scholarship (or admission to a certain prized school) that everyone forgets the student will be far from home for the first time and will no longer hear the cheers of his family at every game; no small matter when this support may be at the heart of his athletic experience. At its worst, homesickness can cause a student-athlete to drop out – a real tragedy for the student and a significant one for the coach and team.

The point here is not whether growing up involves knowing how to be independent. Certainly, it does, but some students are simply not ready. If they have a bad experience first time out in college, they may never make the break to mature adulthood.

Obviously, thousands of students make this transition without any trouble. One athletic director said some student-athletes can hardly wait to get away from well-meaning but domineering parents who second-guess their and the coaches' every move.

Take time to know where you honestly fit into this picture.

Dealing With Stress

Suppose you get a sports scholarship of some kind. You and your parents need to realize that such a situation puts stress on you to produce results. Can you handle this?

Parents of a high school track star turned down a sports scholarship for their daughter because they did not want her to feel she ever had to put sports above academics. The pressure she might impose on herself concerned them, and this was part of a family discussion. Her sports talents still helped her gain admission to the university, where she is a member of the track team.

Each family is different. Not all can afford to turn down scholarship help. The lesson here is that families need to understand each other. What one student can handle, another may not be able to manage.

Understand Financial Aid

There is one place in the process where family preparation is vital and can pay off. Much of the assistance for student-athletes includes at least some need-based aid. This is a vital part of your financial planning for college.

Quite simply, "need" is the difference between what it costs to attend a college and what your family can afford to contribute toward your education. The calculation sounds simple, but it can only be made if the college's financial aid office has all the figures it needs to work with. They know the top line – how much it costs to attend – but you and your family have to supply the bottom line.

That means starting early, because financial aid often is on a first-come, first-served basis. Get a good book on financial aid and learn the ins and outs of financial aid forms. Many factors enter into this equation – not only assets such as the value of your bank account but "liabilities" such as the number of brothers and sisters of college age. You should have backup materials, including copies of tax returns, readily at hand. For a detailed examination of the financial aid process, get *Don't Miss Out* ($10.00 postpaid) by Anna and Robert Leider (to order, see inside back cover).

You can still receive an athletic grant-in-aid or partial scholarship even if your family's contribution is substantial.

And remember that some of the Division III schools, where all aid is based on need, are very expensive. You may be eligible for assistance even if your family is prepared to be a lot of help.

File early! College after college echoes these words. Financial aid funds are limited, especially at some smaller schools, and it is often the case of the early applicant getting the financial dollar. It's up to your family to see that you are at the front of the line.

Nobody says this is going to be easy, but some honest discussion is bound to pay off for both you and your parents. They can help you find the best place for you and your sport. Then it's up to you to make the most of it.

Guidance Counselors — Part of the Team

6

Your guidance counselor is another key player in your search for the winning edge. Chances are he or she is trying to serve the needs of many students and helping you with your college search is just one of his or her duties. This means you must take responsibility for letting your counselor know exactly what help you need. Your coach, counselor and parents are all there to help you, not carry the ball for you. Take the initiative early on. Develop a relationship with your counselor and encourage one or both of your parents to meet your counselor as well.

College Resources

Your guidance counselor has information available to help you make choices. As the two of you work together through your high school career, your counselor will be the key resource for helping you match your academic talents with the right colleges. Some larger high schools have career and college centers with computer programs devoted to college information. If you have a computer at home, you can surf the Internet until you feel as though you've toured the entire universe of schools. If you don't have that kind of computer access, your guidance counselor still should have books and manuals to start you on the way.

Start Early

"Start early" is the advice given by absolutely everyone. Guidance counselors shake their heads in frustration when students rush in at the last minute. For anyone wanting sports scholarships, it's impossible.

What constitutes early? At many high schools, your counselor remains with you throughout your high school career, so if you have a plan, mention it during your freshman year. Otherwise, the best time to start planning is sophomore year; waiting until junior year is pushing your luck.

Your goals may change from what they were in your sophomore year, but if your guidance counselor gets to know you, he or she can begin to do exactly what the title implies – "guide" you through the process.

Don't Forget Academics

Don't forget a major function of the counselor – to help you choose courses that will provide the right foundation for your college career. That's the correct thing to do – and the NCAA rules demand it. You must have taken the right "core" academic courses to even be eligible for a scholarship. And you can't catch up on three years of neglect in your senior year.

Former Washington Redskin Dexter Manley's courageous confession that he couldn't read despite having graduated from Oklahoma State University won't change such tragedies overnight, but more and more people are concerned.

Prodded by U.S. Senator Bill Bradley of New Jersey and others, the NCAA began publicly disclosing graduation rates and other pertinent information before a federal law (the Student Right-to-Know and Campus Security Act) forced it to. Key figures for Division I schools are included in our charts and discussed in Chapter 1. Even more detail is available in the full NCAA report, a copy of which has been sent to every high school guidance department. Check out the schools that interest you. You will find breakdowns by individual sports and by racial groups. There also is information on the grade averages and test scores of recruited athletes and a listing of academic majors of the athletes. (Ask your counselor for help in interpreting these numbers. You'll find, for instance, that graduation rates for students as a whole tend to be lower in urban schools where students may have to drop out to earn money or carry a lighter load because of a job, pushing graduation beyond six years.)

If you are looking at Division II or III schools, be sure to ask the admissions and athletic staff not only about graduations rates, but about how student-athletes stack up alongside the rest of the student body in terms of test scores and other measurements.

Initial-Eligibility Clearinghouse

If you will be making an official visit to a Division I college during your senior year, you'll need some help from your counselor. The NCAA has set up an initial-eligibility clearinghouse to provide colleges with a report on your grades and standardized test scores. Your counselor will have the forms you need – basically, you give your high school and testing services permission to provide transcripts and tests scores to the clearinghouse, which in turn sends them to any college that wants to invite you for a visit. There is an $18 fee for this service. If you have previously been granted a fee waiver for the SAT or ACT, your counselor can authorize a waiver of the clearinghouse fee. If your counselor is not familiar with the clearinghouse, or has run out of registration materials, he or she should call 319/337-1492.

Your Counselor Doesn't Work Alone

Through this entire process, your counselor will be looking to combine two things – a good academic "fit" for you plus the best place for you to use your sports talents. For some students, this means trying for a big name athletic scholarship, for others, it means using athletic skills to help get you into a small prestigious school. To do this effectively, counselors must consult with specialists regarding many of their students. A young violinist in the school orchestra may want to use her or his musical talent in the same way you want to use your athletic ability. The guidance counselor consults an expert – the music teacher– for information about the student's chances.

In your case, the counselor will work with your coach, first to get his or her evaluation of your talent, and then, ideally, to help get you into the right college with as much financial aid as possible. We will go into specifics on the admission application process in a later chapter.

Encourage your parents to meet your guidance counselors. Counselors can relieve a lot of stress by providing answers to baffling questions such as, "How do we know what colleges are right for Susie?" They have the computer programs and books, they know the admission process, they know college admission people, and helping students is their business.

Help From the Coach

Your high school coach is often the "go-between" in your search for an athletic scholarship or other financial aid, which means you must work together at every stage of your search. While your coach often holds the key to your sports future, how he or she uses that key depends largely on you.

Coaches want to see their players do well in college. They really like young people or they would not be coaching. Successful college athletes also bring them credit and validate their coaching skills. But a coach can be a very busy person. You are going to be asking her or him to do even more. So it will be good for you to do some groundwork.

Laying the Groundwork — Your Sophomore Year

It should go without saying that developing a good relationship with your high school coach is most important if you hope to continue your athletic career. If you have been a disruptive, rebellious member of a team – in and out of the coach's doghouse – do you really expect that coach to go the extra mile to help you get into college or win some financial aid?

You should level with your coach about your ambitions as early as possible. There are always some athletic late-bloomers, but most future college athletes show signs of their abilities by their sophomore year. That's not too early to ask your coach the hard question: "Do you think I have the ability to play college sports?"

The coach's answer may well be a conditional one; for example, "Yes, but only if you improve certain facets of your game." This can be the basis of a frank and continuing dialogue. A coach does you no favor by building up your hopes and expectations beyond what your skills merit.

Along with your guidance counselor and your parents, the coach plays a key role in your initial narrowing down of possible colleges. Even at this early state, it's a complicated mix of considerations. The sports program should be within range of your athletic abilities, taking into account the improvement two more years of competition and physical maturity will bring. The academic program should be within reach of your scholastic abilities. (What do your grades show you can handle?) The size of the college and its distance from home should also be within the scope you think is best for you.

Many factors still can change. In your junior year, for example, your higher-than-expected PSAT score suggests more academic opportunities; your sudden growth spurt makes you a better athlete; your curve ball finds the strike zone instead of the dirt. Allowances can be made for changes, but it's hard to recover from a tardy start.

This is the time for an early dose of reality. Your sports skills may be good enough to get you onto the playing fields of Amherst, Williams or some other prestigious small college. But your grades aren't in the same league. On the other hand, your grades may gain you admission to the University of Nebraska, but your sports skills won't get you off the bench.

The solution? Find some schools in the middle that fit your academic and sports profile. Remember, you are not locking in a final choice here, just selecting some terrain for further exploration.

Preliminary Inquiries — Your Sophomore Year

Your sophomore year is a good time to make preliminary inquiries about colleges that interest you. A brief letter to the coach indicating interest in his or her school and sport is appropriate. Later you will be preparing more detailed forms of communication, but some basic rules apply to both undertakings.

Be sure you have the right coach's name and that you spell it correctly. Nothing will help a letter find the wastebasket quicker than a wrong name. College coaches are a movable lot, so this book has not tried to list names. That might do you more harm than good. Instead, it includes telephone numbers for athletic departments in every institution in the NAIA and all divisions of the NCAA. Call before you write!

Your first letter also should demonstrate some knowledge of that college's sports program. If the school has won a conference championship or other honor, mention it in your letter. You don't need to go into detail about your athletic skills at this stage. You are only a sophomore, and have a lot of growing and learning to do. It is appropriate to mention that you will be looking for financial aid down the road.

Don't expect great things from this first approach. At most you will probably get a sports brochure or media guide and a current schedule. But your name will go into a file, and who knows, a college recruiter checking out another athlete may cast an eye in your direction.

Refining the List — Your Junior Year

Your junior year is the time to begin making some serious decisions, and refine your list. Your athletic skills should be more fully developed, so you and your coach can make a more realistic assessment of how your game will stack up for college. Can you be a Division I athlete, Division II, Division III?

The same thing holds true on the academic side. Your PSAT scores should give you some idea of how you will do on the SAT. If your scores were lower than expected, you might consider a prep course before you take the test that counts. If possible, take the SAT (or the ACT, if that's what the colleges you are interested in prefer) more than once to get the best possible score.

You also will be refining your goals in life and, with the help of your guidance counselor, tailoring your high school schedule to support those goals. These absolutely must include the 13 "core" courses required if you are to receive an athletic scholarship at an NCAA school – three years of English, two of mathematics, two of social sciences, two of natural or physical sciences (including one lab course), two additional years in English or natural or physical sciences and two additional years in any of the above fields or in foreign language, computer science, philosophy or nondoctrinal (comparative) religion.

The requirements vary slightly if you're entering Division I schools: you must have four years of English, and only one additional year in English or natural or physical sciences. Furthermore, your math courses must include a year of algebra and a year of geometry.

Few students can accurately map out their futures at this point. But you should start to see some patterns. Maybe you have found you really like math and science after all. On the other hand, science courses may leave you cold while English literature fascinates you. You will be working with your guidance counselor to make the most of these new goals. While making sure you study all the fundamentals, you should add advanced classes whenever possible.

Just as your evolving athletic skills are influencing your choice of schools, so should your career inclination. If you want to study science or engineering, you should take a harder look at colleges with strong programs in those fields. You also will be aware that lab courses take a lot of time, and so does sports practice. You'll have to start thinking about how best to balance these future demands on your time.

A warning: as you narrow your list of schools, you and your counselors should note any special entrance requirements. Do you need two years of a foreign language? Do you have to take achievement tests in certain subjects? It would be a shame to pick the perfect college – for both sports and academics – and then be turned down for admission because you are missing a course or a test.

The Athletic Resume — Your Junior Year

During your junior year, you should approach selected college coaches seriously. You've followed some schools more closely than others, and your letter should reflect that familiarity. Before you write, call the school to make sure you have the right coach – there may have been a change. And spell his or her name correctly.

Appendix A contains a sample sports resume. This is an excellent way to provide information to college personnel who are receiving hundreds of letters from prospective students.

Some student-athletes begin sending such resumes in their sophomore year. At the sophomore level, your cover letter should be a simple indication of interest.

As you get closer to decision time, your letter should tell the coach why you are considering that college. Go beyond your interest in the sports program and explain how the school will help you realize your overall goals. You should also tell the coach how you think you could be an asset to her or his program. You should indicate you will need a scholarship or other financial aid and inquire about that availability.

Most importantly, you need a letter of recommendation from your high school coach that tells the college coach what you can contribute to the program. Your high school coach should go beyond your physical skills, important as those are, and emphasize the intangibles – your work and practice habits, your sportsmanship, your inspiration to others on the team. We cannot stress enough the importance of your high school coach's support in getting a college interested.

The college coach's response will necessarily be limited. In Division I and II schools, she or he cannot phone you, accept a collect call from you or make personal contact with you off the college campus until July 1 following your junior year (or August 15 for football). In Division III, schools can contact you anytime after you finish your Junior year. Coaches can, however, write you, and there's nothing to bar your talking to them while on an unofficial visit to the campus.

A caution: Many college coaches told us that the letters they get from high school coaches are mostly sheer puff. If the athlete was really that good, she or he would already be in the Hall of Fame instead of looking for a college scholarship. Talk to your coach before he or she writes the letter. It should be as specific as possible – citing your accomplishments and potential. But it should also be realistic – and not paint a picture of you that your sports skills can't back up.

Your coach's role does not end with these letters. He or she will be the point person if and when you attract a college's interest. Your coach may get phone calls from the college coach (or an assistant) inquiring about your progress. Maintaining that interest, once expressed, is very important. Make sure your coach knows you appreciate the help.

What should you do if your high school coach changes jobs, and you are left with someone who's just met you for the first time? Use your former coach for a reference, by all means, but don't be afraid to talk to another coach in your area or conference – someone who has seen you play for a couple of years. They may be glad to help. Meanwhile, you should establish a relationship with your new coach.

Along with the letters and your athletic resume, you might also include a transcript of your academic record up to that point. Be sure to keep college coaches up-to-date on where and when you will be competing. And that means not only your regular high school schedule, but any summer league games or tournaments as well. The college coach may not drop by to see you personally, but he or she almost surely has some scouts out there.

Final Play — Your Senior Year

The summer between your junior and senior years is your last chance to showcase your skills at sports camps, clinics or in summer leagues. If a school high on your list has expressed interest and has a sports camp, you should attend if at all possible. Otherwise, you need your coach's advice and counsel on how to make this last shot an effective one.

Randy Lambert, athletic director and men's basketball coach at Division III Maryville College, prepared a list of suggestions for high school coaches to use in helping their athletes attract the attention of Division III sports staffs. A brief summary of these suggestions may give you a basis on which to judge what your own coach is doing to help you and your classmates:

* Meet area Division III coaches, attend games, study their program and know the kind of athletes they need and want.

- Distribute an annual mail-out to Division III coaches about the senior athletes who are or may be valid prospects. Inform the interested coaches regularly through newsletters or phone calls about the prospect's seasonal progress.
- Keep a file on each senior athlete containing vital information.
- Work closely with the guidance office to supervise the athlete's academic performance.
- Make sure the athlete is completing the ACT and/or SAT tests in his or her junior year.
- Alert your senior athletes and check on their completion of the standardized financial aid applications.
- Have game films available to send to college coaches.
- Maintain a checklist of your senior athletes' progress toward college admission. (Appendix B of this book)

About Those Videos

More and more student-athletes are sending videotapes along with their letters. Almost all college coaches we talked with welcome tapes. But remember, coaches are busy people and will probably get hundreds of tapes to review. So keep yours short and to the point.

Tapes need not feature Academy Award-winning cinematography, but they should be clear and sharp. In other words, edit out all extraneous scenes and keep it under five minutes. For team sports, include some "half-court" scenes, preferably from a high vantage point, showing how you move on the field and work with your teammates. You will also need some close-ups to demonstrate your mastery of the sport's fundamentals – hitting, throwing, running, stick-handling, whatever.

Another good tip from Coach Lambert: When sending game or meet videos, take nothing for granted. Be sure to include your uniform number (or other identifying mark) to avoid any possible confusion. Use standard VHS-format tapes.

Videos can be great, but they do not take the place of talent-indicating statistics and a strong recommendation from your coach. As a leading college golf coach noted, a video without some low scores and high tournament finishes is just another pretty picture. Another coach remembers a tape of a woman basketball player with her movements beautifully choreographed to classical music. She still remembers the tape – but isn't sure what happened to the player.

College Nights

Coaches at your high school also might consider sponsoring an athletic "College Night," a plan that works successfully for Dan Meier, a football coach and guidance counselor in Northern Virginia. Each December, Coach Meier (working with other high school coaches), invites representatives from more than 65 area colleges to meet with senior student-athletes from 40 area high schools. This allows easy an exchange of information for parents and students as admission and financial aid application deadlines near.

Tips for Campus Visits

Once you have a list of colleges that look like good matches for you, you should plan some campus visits. Of course, many of your questions could easily be answered with a quick phone call, but nothing takes the place of a personal visit to get a true picture of the school.

Remember the Rules

There are some rules about visiting colleges that may or may not apply in your case.

- Your "official" expense-paid visit – in other words, the college is recruiting you – may not be made before you start classes in your senior year. You can make just one such visit to a school, and only five total official visits to NCAA Division I and Division II schools.
- You cannot make an official visit to a Division I or II college until you have supplied the school with a score from one of the standardized tests – SAT, PSAT, PACT-Plus or ACT and a copy of your academic transcript. (As mentioned earlier, an initial-eligibility clearinghouse has been set up to certify your scores and grades. Ask your guidance counselor about this.)
- You may visit a college as many times as you wish as long as you and your parents are picking up the tab. Take care, however, not to schedule your visit during one of the "dead" periods when contacts with coaches are prohibited. On your unofficial visits, the school can give you up to three complimentary tickets to an on-campus athletic event. In Division II and III, schools can also pay for one meal at an on-campus dining facility. But you and your parents cannot be "wined and dined." Even on the official visit there are some restrictions on how lavish the hospitality can be.

Be aware of the rules (see Chapter 2). They are very specific and such seemingly trivial things as gifts of caps or T-shirts (bearing college logos) have gotten schools, and prospective student-athletes, in hot water. Don't leave your parents out of this process. A recent NCAA infraction involved a college head coach who had contact with a prospect before a competition. The prospect's mother had told the coach it was a practice.

Rules aside – and that doesn't mean to ignore or bend them – college visits are still the best way to judge a college and its athletic program. This sounds like plain old common sense – and it is. But timing your college visits, so they do you the most good, may be more of a problem than you first realize.

Planning Your Visit

Ideally, you can learn a lot from going to a practice in your sport. Most important, you can watch the coach or coaches in action to see how they run the show. Can you take the "drill sergeant" approach? Screaming and yelling works fine with some students, but it's not everybody's style. Part of the reason for your visit is to eliminate as many unpleasant surprises as possible if you should choose to attend a particular college.

Attending a practice is a fine idea, but it may be difficult. Your high school season and the college's may run at the same time – football, most definitely, but it's true for most other sports as well.

Can you get away to make college visits? All the more reason to establish a good rapport with your high school coach. Ask her or him to work out a "game plan" that allows you to help the team while giving you time to visit colleges. That's another argument for an early start. Don't get caught in your senior year committing yourself to a college and a sports program about which you know almost nothing.

You may learn something very revealing in your first telephone call to a college. Don't be afraid to "trouble" someone with a call. If you find the athletic department folk are too busy to talk to you, you may rightly decide that this isn't a place with students' interests in mind.

Chemistry – that certain something – is a big part of romance and plays a part in college selection, too. One student-athlete's family tells of a campus visit where the coach was late, appeared bored, and failed to introduce the student to other athletes on a facilities walk-around. The student ruled out that college on the spot, and subsequent calls of apology from the coach when he discovered he'd had a top-ranking runner in his grasp just made it worse.

Another critical factor is your first-hand impression of a school. That's why visiting when the school is in session is so vital.

Talk to members of the team, though you have to be a little careful there. They are only human; they may or may not want to encourage you for reasons of their own – more competition for their positions, for instance. Still, you need to check them out. You should be immediately suspicious, warns one leading coach, if the staff tries to steer you away from talking to players.

Don't limit your visits to the athletic field. Walk around, talk to other students. Find out about other aspects of student life. The athletic director of a small college in a small Midwestern town advises prospective student-athletes to go to the cafeteria and talk to a variety of students (you also might want to sample the cuisine). He pointed out since a small town doesn't usually have much to offer in the way of restaurants and cultural activities, you need to make sure a college in such a place provides enough social facilities to suit you.

If you are visiting a university, allow time to cover all the territory. Pick up copies of the university newspaper and any independent publications you find.

Ask Questions

Here are some specific questions to ask the athletic department before you decide to apply. We suggest you prepare a checklist of these questions so you can compare answers from each college.

1. How much time – both hours per day and months per year – will you be expected to spend on the practice field? Be sure the balance between sports time and class time is not going to put you in an academic bind. NCAA rules restrict practice time to 20 hours a week, give student-athletes one day a week off, and limit the hours that may be spent traveling to and from games. The NCAA has also reduced the length of Division I and Division II seasons in all sports except football. Still, this may be more than you can afford to spend.

2. What support services are available? Are there study halls, independent counselors, tutors? Can you expect to pursue your chosen course of study and still have time for sports?

3. How many athletes graduate? What are the grade point averages on the team? Their majors? If all or most are physical education majors, are they being pushed in that direction?

4. Where do the athletes live? Athletic dorms have been banned at NCAA schools since 1996. Training table meals also are now restricted to one a day during the regular academic year. So what is the school doing to replace these once-popular perks?

5. What happens if you get hurt? The NCAA won't let colleges give ironclad promises that financial aid will continue, but what has the school's policy been? Also, ask for examples of how the school treats injured athletes.

6. How is the team shaping up for the years ahead and how will you fit into the picture? Are there a host of other players at your position or do you fill a pressing need? How soon can you realistically expect to play?

7. Is the overall athletic program financially healthy? Is there any chance your sport could be dropped entirely before you graduate?

8. Are there any special weight restrictions that could be harmful to your health? Surveys show an increase in reported eating disorders (anorexia nervosa and bulimia) in some sports, notably wrestling, gymnastics, skiing, track, cross country, football and swimming. More institutions need to follow the lead of the University of Texas at Austin and the University of Washington in developing programs of nutrition and education for dealing with eating disorders in athletics.

9. If your sport is considered a "minor" one at the college you are considering (you can hardly call lacrosse a minor sport if the team is its division's national champion, for instance), what are the qualifications of the coach? Is it his or her turn to coach (inwardly kicking and screaming) the volleyball team? Does the coach really know the game? Enough athletic directors mentioned this in interviews that it's worth your time to check.

10. This is even trickier, but try to find out if the coach and any staff members in your sport are planning to leave. Some coaches seem to be on the list any time a college vacancy opens up, which should give you a signal. There are no guarantees, but occasionally this may save you some disappointment. Sports editors at the college or local newspapers may be able to help you with this information.

11. For men, is your sport one that might be dropped or downgraded to club status as the college tries to meet the terms of Title IX (see Chapter 2)? For women, how is the school moving toward full compliance with Title IX? Is

it being dragged along in the face of possible legal action or are school officials actively seeking to upgrade their women's sports program?

For the next few years, students entering colleges will be faced with several complicated issues – gender equity, reform, certification, even AIDS education.

College sports must deal with HIV prevention and education as does professional sports and the general public. The NCAA's Committee on Competitive Safeguards and Medical Aspects of Sports provides member schools with brochures on AIDS education and a guideline memo (based on common sense and basic hygiene), regarding blood on uniforms and equipment. Concern is obviously ongoing, but there is no need for panic. The chance of contracting HIV from sports contact is extremely low, but feel free to ask any college's sports representatives how they are dealing with this question.

The answers you get to all these questions will help you as you juggle all your options. Big schools may have more support services for their athletes, but they may also demand more of your time. Small schools, on the other hand, may offer fewer services but a closer relationship with your professors, making such services less necessary. The choices are difficult. But armed with all you have learned, now is the time to make the final cut and establish a list of colleges where you feel comfortable both athletically and academically.

Time to Decide

At long last, all the work you, your family, your coach and your counselor have done should start paying happy dividends. If not, memories of this experience may make visits to the dentist seem pain-free and fun.

If you have been following the advice in this book, you will have been making a list of prospective colleges all along. Most important, you have faced reality and, though perhaps including a "go for it" gamble, eliminated the impossible.

You know what you can do in your sport. You have an honest idea of what schools fit both your talent and desire. You have prepared your academic work and taken all the tests. You've been contacting coaches and working with your high school coach to get the attention of college athletic departments.

You've completed all your financial forms, and made copies for your files. (A high school financial aid counselor tells horror stories of students whose forms were lost by colleges, and the students had no backups.)

You have also visited some colleges. You have some dreams in your head about a few of them. Now it's time for some tough decisions.

Wedding Bells?

Remember, it takes two to make a marriage. You may have fallen in love with a particular school but found the feeling was not reciprocated. Admissions and athletic department staffers may have been cordial and polite, but they were definitely lacking in passion. Elsewhere, the situation may have been reversed. You were not impressed by the college and its programs, but its recruiters seem genuinely interested in you. What do you do?

For one thing, don't put all your hopes into one college application. By all means, apply to your first love, but give yourself some other choices, too.

One top coach suggests you concentrate on three schools, plus a backup; any more can be confusing.

Assessing Your Chances

Even if you're not a blue-chipper, you may have gotten some sign of acceptance from college coaches. Try to pin this down as much as possible.

A coach who has been encouraging about your prospects may have been just as encouraging to dozens of others. Consider the coach's perspective. He or she needs players for particular positions, to fill graduation vacancies or to shore up weak spots on the team. So do hundreds of other schools.

The coach may well have a short list of players he or she passionately wants. But just like you, coaches also need some backups. It is to their advantage – although not always to yours – to keep as many prospects interested as they can until decision day.

The moral: Get something in writing if you can. Highly recruited athletes will surely be asked to sign a National Letter of Intent. Such letters are recognized by most major conferences and bind a player to a school. The player cannot back out without penalty. Signing dates vary with the sport, but always come after the end of that sport's season.

If you are not in the sought-after group, you may still be able to get some less formal commitment from a college about admission and financial aid. Division III schools, for example, don't permit athletic letters of intent, but admission officers often write letters to prospective students before the official notification date saying, in effect, that they are holding a spot for you. So long as this is done for students generally – not just for athletes – it is perfectly within the rules.

Your coach and guidance counselor also may be talking to college coaches, admission people and financial aid officers. Their contacts should be helpful in evaluating your chances at a particular school.

The Application and Follow-up

So we come down to your formal application. Get the forms early and understand what is required. Some colleges ask for one or more essays. Don't wait until the last minute to start composing and write at least two drafts. As with financial forms, make copies. Mail your application, along with recommendations from your counselors and a transcript of your grades, as early as possible.

Call the coaches you have been working with to let them know you have applied. In many Division III schools, for example, the coach has no formal role in the admission process, but there is nothing to stop her or him from inquiring about whether your application has arrived. Such expressions of interest can often help move your application into the "accepted" pile. A coach's interest also can help make sure your financial aid application does not get left on the sidelines.

The Decision

The Final Four of decisions comes after you hear from colleges. This can be a happy time if the news is good, and your "problem" is deciding between two or three equally attractive institutions.

Unfortunately, life also can be cruel. A desirable college may admit you, but without any promise of an athletic scholarship or other financial aid. Your only offer may be from the college at the bottom of your list or – a worst case scenario – no offers at all arrive in your mailbox. What do you do then?

Although all the schools you applied to should have some attraction, you still may have your heart set on your top choice. That is understandable. So do you accept the aid offer from the less-favored school anyway? That is a decision only you, your parents and your advisers can make.

Relax a bit by talking to some of your friends who are in college. Chances are, those who didn't get into their first choice school are perfectly happy now and wonder why they wasted time worrying.

There are some other options, of course. For example:

- You could attend a community college or junior college for a year or two and start the search for a scholarship all over again. Although this book concentrates on four-year colleges, junior colleges can have excellent sports programs – and also can be great places to flesh out your academic record. To learn more about the 540 members of the National Junior College Athletic Association (NJCAA), write NJCAA, PO Box 7305, Colorado Springs, CO 80933, http://www.njcaa.org.
- If your family finances permit, you could go to the favored school that denied you a scholarship and take a swing at your sport as a walk-on. Many schools, especially the smaller ones, still encourage non-scholarship players to try out for the team. Perhaps if you prove yourself, a scholarship or other aid can be arranged for future years.

A wrong decision is not the end of the world, although you may have to pay some penalties. Athletes who sign a National Letter of Intent and then change their minds will lose, in almost all cases, two years of eligibility. So be sure before you sign anything.

Athletes who transfer from one four-year school to another don't lose eligibility, but they must sit out a year before they can play again.

College sports is a wide, wide world. We have concentrated on intercollegiate varsity sports, but they are just the tip of the athletic iceberg. Even if you do not get an athletic scholarship, or make varsity as a walk-on, your playing days need not be over.

Club sports are very popular in many schools. Although normally run by students and not by athletic departments (that's the rule in NCAA Division I schools), clubs can be very competitive. They play against other colleges and have good coaches. In a few rare cases, some offer financial aid.

If the school does not have club sports, you can always find intramural games. Most colleges have extensive programs in almost any sport you can name.

So here's to you and college sports, whichever way the ball bounces!

The Winning Edge

This book aims to help you use your sport to obtain the best college education possible—an education that includes good sportsmanship and a fun social life, as well as the rigors of academics.

But use your sport, don't be used by it, no matter what level of play or financial aid it gets you. If a great scholarship means you spend so much time playing big-time college sports that you don't graduate, you haven't ended up with much. A very small percentage of student-athletes make the pros, and of those, most have short careers. The cheering and the big money soon stop.

As Charles B. Reed, chancellor of the State University of Florida System, said at one of the NCAA's annual meetings: "Your odds of becoming a rock star or an astronaut are about the same as starting for the New York Knicks."

Cedric W. Dempsey, the NCAA's executive director, puts the same sentiment in cold, hard figures:

- There are about one million high school football players about 500,000 basketball players. Of that number, about 150 make it to the NFL and about 50 make an NBA team.
- Less than 3 percent of college seniors will play one year of professional basketball.
- The odds of a high school football player making it to the pros at all – let alone having a career – are about 6,000 to 1; the odds for a high school basketball player – 10,000 to 1.

Ollie Gelston, retired basketball coach and assistant athletics director at Montclair State University, a Division III school in New Jersey, once wrote: "People say to me that to win is to be successful as a coach. Well, success to me is seeing my kids come back in a three-piece suit. That's success, that's coaching." In his more than 30 years of coaching, 83 percent of Gelston's players earned their degrees – going on to become doctors, dentists, lawyers, teachers and, yes, coaches.

And this attitude is not restricted to small colleges.

Penn State is a perennial football power. Coach Joe Paterno has earned an enviable reputation as a successful coach and teacher. Often asked which has been his best team, Coach Paterno says he cannot answer just yet. "Our best team will be the one that produces the most people who lead active, productive lives in our society."

Do the coaches you have been talking to understand the relationship of sports to the rest of your life? A few worn-out references at a sports awards banquet to "playing the game of life" is not what Coach Paterno is talking about. Don't settle for less. Fortunately, many coaches embrace Paterno's standards and are looking for student-athletes who want to work and learn.

The Winning Edge in College

"The Winning Edge" means many things. Information you find here may give you the winning edge on the path into college, but we hope that is not all.

If taking time to research the right match for you and your skills results in a satisfying college experience, that's a winning edge, too.

You will make lifelong friendships and take away memories of the Big Win over Wossamatta U. on club teams as well as the varsity. You can make lifelong friendships and take away memories of the Big Win over Phi Fratta Fratta on intramural teams. To the surprise of many athletes, you also can make lifelong friendships and take away memories of the Big Win over James Joyce's *Ulysses* in a college English classroom.

Although admission officers won't say so on the record, successful student-athletes have a bit of a winning edge in getting into some of the most selective graduate programs. Just as colleges are looking for "involved" students – musicians, student leaders and others as well as athletes – so are graduate schools. Your demonstrated ability to compete on the playing fields adds shine to your classroom performance.

Studies show that despite some tragic examples in big-time football and basketball, student-athletes have a higher graduation rate than the total school population.

The Winning Edge in Life

Being on a team should teach you the importance of discipline, hard work, practice, personal responsibility, giving up personal glory for the team good, how to win and how to lose; ingredients for success in any field.

Mike Mullan coaches men's tennis at Division III Swarthmore College and recently served on the NCAA Men's and Women's Tennis Committee. Writing in the NCAA News, Mullan comments on the lessons sports can teach about society:

"Participation on a college sports team in the 1990s has some congruency with the way work is organized in our complex modern society. Players learn quickly that achievement in sports is not reducible to simple formulas – skill is a process that is guaranteed to be frustrating, with its many small successes and failures.

"In modern work, the way people get along is also important. On an individual level, the person who has learned to strive hard yet coexist with workers, who has the skills and disposition to pull together diverse sources of information and the ability to absorb temporary setbacks, has a leg up in an economy that stresses communications over production.

"At Swarthmore, over one-third of the student body plays a varsity sport. There are teams that experience championship moments and those whose records are sprinkled with more losses than wins; yet, I have to feel that all the students who play sports are learning implicit lessons about working in complex, modern organizations."

Yale University's sports brochures follow a "Path of Giants" theme, featuring not only on-field honors but the career and professional successes achieved by former team members as well.

Lifetime habits of exercise and nutrition can give you a real winning edge for years to come. More than one college refers to its "Life Sports" program, and most provide fitness equipment and training plus nutritional guidance for its athletes. Juvenal, a Roman poet who lived in the first century A.D., wrote "Orandum est ut sit mens sana in corpore sano" – "You should pray for a sound mind in a sound body." That often-quoted phrase describes the completely educated person.

We've called it "The Winning Edge."

Section II

Winning Teams and Coaches Advice

BASEBALL

- **NCAA Division I champions:** 1996-97 and 1995-96, Louisiana State; 1994-95, Cal State Fullerton; 1993-94, Oklahoma; 1992-93, Louisiana State; 1991-92, Pepperdine; 1990-91, Louisiana State; 1989-90, Georgia; 1988-89, Wichita State; other past champions include Stanford, Arizona, Miami, Texas, Arizona State and Southern Cal.
- **NCAA Division II champions:** 1996-97, Cal State Chico; 1995-96, Kennesaw State; 1994-95, Florida Southern (eighth championship); 1993-94, Central Missouri State; 1992-93 and 1991-92, Tampa; 1990-91 and 1989-90, Jacksonville State; 1988-89, Cal Poly San Luis Obispo; other past champions include, Troy State, Cal State Northridge, Cal Poly Pomona and University of California Riverside.
- **NCAA Division III champions:** 1996-97, Southern Maine; 1995-96, William Patterson; 1994-95, La Verne; 1993-94, Wisconsin-Oshkosh; 1992-93, Montclair State; 1991-92, William Paterson; 1990-91, Southern Maine; 1989-90, Eastern Connecticut State; 1988-89, North Carolina Wesleyan; other past champions include Ithaca, Marietta, and Ramapo.
- **NAIA champions:** 1996-97, Brewton-Parker (GA); 1995-96, Lewis and Clark State (ID); 1994-95, Bellevue (NE); 1993-94, Kennesaw State (GA); 1992-93, St. Francis (IL); 1991-92, Lewis and Clark State (fourth title in a row).

People Are the Secret

from Gene Stephenson, Baseball Coach, Wichita State University

When visiting a college, the *people*–not the facilities–should be your foremost concern. Meet the people you are going to be around–players, coaches, instructors. Then ask yourself this question: Are they people with whom I want to spend the next four years of my life?

Getting ready to play college sports takes a lot of work. Summer leagues are a big help and so are sports camps. But, remember that the summer after your sophomore year is probably the earliest in terms of physical maturity. The summer after your junior year is when college coaches really start looking. If the college you have your eye on has a camp, attend it if at all possible. At least 25 percent of our players attended the Wichita State camp.

In evaluating your baseball skills, don't forget about the professional scouts. If one has seen you play, ask him–or have your coach ask him–at what level he thinks you can play. When contacting college coaches, be sure to tell them what scouts have seen you in action. And be sure the coaches know your schedule, summer league as well as regular season.

Be flexible in what you expect in a grant-in-aid. No baseball player at Wichita State in my years has ever been on a full scholarship–although I think all of them deserved one. Our College World Series champions, however, had 27 players receiving some aid. We re-examine scholarships every year and improve them to reflect the players' value to the team. So if an offer for your freshman year seems small, remember you'll have a chance to prove your worth.

Finally, work hard on all phases of your life by habit. By that I mean be the best you can be–by habit–in anything for which you are responsible. People who do that as a way of life are not faced with having to come up with a special effort in critical situations, they do it every day as a matter of habit.

Gene Stephenson's Shockers won the College World Series in 1989, were runners-up in 1993, 1991 and 1982 and finished third in 1988. He was named Coach of the Year in 1982.

BASKETBALL

Men

NCAA Division I champions: 1996-97 and 1995-96, Kentucky; 1994-95, UCLA (10th title); 1993-94, Arkansas; 1992-93, North Carolina; 1991-92 and 1990-91, Duke; 1989-90, Nevada-Las Vegas; 1988-89, Michigan; other past champions include Kansas, Indiana, Villanova, Georgetown, North Carolina State, Louisville, Michigan State and Marquette.

NCAA Division II champions: 1996-97, Cal State Bakersfield; 1995-96, Fort Hays State; 1994-95, Southern Indiana; 1993-94 and 1992-93, Cal State-Bakersfield; 1991-92, Virginia Union; 1990-91, University of North Alabama; 1989-90, Kentucky Wesleyan; 1988-89, North Carolina Central; other past champions include Lowell, Sacred Heart, Jacksonville State, Central Missouri State and Wright State.

NCAA Division III champions: 1996-97, Illinois Wesleyan; 1995-96, Rowan; 1994-95, University of Wisconsin-Platteville (undefeated season); 1993-94, Lebanon Valley; 1992-93, Ohio Northern; 1991-92, Calvin College; 1990-91, University of Wisconsin-Platteville; 1989-90, Rochester; 1988-89, Wisconsin-Whitewater; other past champions include Ohio Wesleyan, North Park, Potsdam State, Scranton and Wabash.

NAIA Division I champions: 1996-97, Life (GA); 1995-96, Oklahoma City; 1994-95, Birmingham-Southern; 1993-94, Oklahoma City; 1992-93, Hawaii Pacific; 1991-92 and 1990-91, Oklahoma City; 1989-90, Birmingham-Southern; 1988-89, St. Mary's (TX).

NAIA Division II champions: 1996-97, Bethel (IN); 1995-96, Albertson (ID); 1994-95, Bethel; 1993-94, Eureka (IL); 1992-93, Willamette; 1991-92, Grace (IN).

Women

NCAA Division I champions: 1996-97, Tennessee (second title in a row); 1994-95, Connecticut (undefeated season); 1993-94, North Carolina; 1992-93, Texas Tech; 1991-92, Stanford; 1990-91, Tennessee; 1989-90, Stanford; 1988-89, Tennessee; other past champions include Louisiana Tech, Texas, Old Dominion and Southern Cal.

NCAA Division II champions: 1996-97, North Dakota; 1995-96, North Dakota State (fourth straight title); 1991-92, Delta State; 1990-91, North Dakota State; 1989-90 and 1988-89, Delta State; other past champions include Hampton, New Haven, Cal Poly Pomona, Central Missouri State and Virginia Union.

NCAA Division III champions: 1996-97, New York University; 1995-96, Wisconsin-Oshkosh; 1994-95 and 1993-94, Capital University (OH); 1992-93, Central (IO); 1991-92, Alma College; 1990-91, St. Thomas (MN); 1989-90, Hope; 1988-89, Elizabethtown; other past champions include Concordia-Moorhead, Wisconsin-Stevens Point, Salem State, Scranton, Rust and North Central.

NAIA Division I champions: 1996-97, Southern Nazarene (OK) (fourth straight tile); 1992-93 and 1991-92, Arkansas Tech; 1990-91, Fort Hays State; 1989-90, Southwestern Oklahoma; 1988-89, Southern Nazarene.

NAIA Division II champions: 1996-97, Northwest Nazarene (ID); 1995-96, Western Oregon (second straight title); 1993-94, Northern State (SD), 1992-93, Northern Montana; 1991-92, Northern State.

Never Say "I Wish I Had"

from Yvonne Kauffman, Women's Basketball Coach, Elizabethtown College

I have a motto I give to my teams: Never have to look at something and say "I wish I had." Be able to look back and say "I did."

That is as true for choosing a college and a sports program as it is for anything else in life. Do what feels right for you. If it doesn't work out and you are not happy, get out. There is nothing wrong with making a mistake so long as you do something to change it.

Of course you should not go into the selection process planning to make a mistake. There are some important steps you should take in making your choice. Make a checklist and rate all the schools on the same points.

First, visit the campus if at all possible. Meet the coach face to face. It really helps the coach to associate a face with a name. If you can't visit, a videotape is the next best thing. But keep it short. When your high school coach writes to recommend you, try to see that the letter accurately assesses your abilities. Too many are just puff. College coaches don't pay much attention to those.

Look at the academics first. You can only play basketball for four years, but your education is for life.

By all means watch the team play. Do you like the style of play? The uniforms? Is the coach a yeller and screamer or the quiet type? Could you play for her or him? Be wary of coaches who promise you too much.

Ask yourself what you really want. Do you need to be a star? A starter your first year? Or do you just want to be on a winning team? You should understand that if the team is in the playoffs regularly you may have to wait your turn to play. If being a star right away is more important, then you should look elsewhere. On the other hand, there are players who don't care that much about winning. They just want to be on a team. There are programs for them, too.

Finally, weigh the financial aid package carefully. It's great to be able to say you are on a basketball scholarship, but a need-based package at a Division III school could amount to more over your four years.

And then do what you have to do.

Yvonne Kauffman's Lady Jays were Division III national champions in 1988-89 and 1981-82.

CREW

Women

> **NCAA National Collegiate champions:** 1996-97, Washington. (Women's rowing was upgraded in 1997 from an "emerging sport" to a full-fledged varsity sport, with its own national championship.)

Men

There is no official NCAA or NAIA championship in men's rowing, but the National Collegiate Rowing Championships are held annually in Cincinnati. Brown, Penn, Yale, Northeastern, Princeton, Washington, Cornell, California, Harvard, Boston University, University of Wisconsin-Madison, Stanford, Rutgers and Dartmouth are among the perennial top teams.

Take a Hard Look at Potential, Commitment

from Buzz Congram, Coach, Northeastern University

Prospective college rowers need to take a hard look at both their own potential and the level of commitment they want to make to the sport. That will make it easier to narrow down a choice of schools. In comparison to other sports, there aren't a lot of crew programs. For those who want to row at the highest level there are the schools in the Eastern Association of Rowing Colleges (EARC) and a group on the West Coast that includes Washington, Cal Berkeley and Stanford. Then there's the Dad Vail League, which has 30-40 schools with smaller programs. And don't forget the schools that have clubs only, if that matches your goals. Almost all the EARC schools, with the exception of the Ivy League, have money for rowers.

Rowing is the kind of sport that relies not only on experienced athletes, but also on those who may have never rowed before. If an athlete has the size and physique, then we will take a chance on teaching the technique. I try to keep some money available for those as well, and to base aid on a combination of need and athletic ability.

Rowing coaches look for size – tall, not a lot of extra body weight – good numbers on ergometer [a sophisticated rowing machine] testing and desire. I rely heavily on the recommendations of high school coaches and rarely see a kid perform, except maybe on videos, which are most welcome. Serious high school rowers should think about trying out for the junior national team. That will involve some ergometer testing under controlled conditions and college coaches watch those carefully.

I don't have a big recruiting budget so I rely on letters I get from interested kids (just pick out several schools that seem to fit your needs and send a letter to "Rowing Coach") and letters I write to coaches. I follow up with phone calls and, if there is mutual interest, we invite them for a campus visit.

Buzz Congram's Northeastern University crews are regularly ranked among the top in the country.

FIELD HOCKEY

NCAA Division I champions: 1996-97, North Carolina (second straight title) ; 1994-95, James Madison; 1993-94, Maryland; 1992-93, 1991-92 and 1990-91, Old Dominion (seven titles in 12 years); 1989-90, North Carolina; 1988-89, Old Dominion; other past champions include Iowa and Connecticut.

NCAA Division II champions: 1996-97, Lock Haven (third straight title); 1993-94, Bloomsburg University of Pennsylvania; 1992-93, Lock Haven; 1991-92, Cal State-Dominguez Hills. (Championships suspended after 1983 season, resumed in 1991.)

NCAA Division III champions: 1996-97, College of New Jersey (formerly Trenton State; second straight title); 1994-95 and 1993-94, Cortland State; 1992-93, William Smith College; 1991-92 and 1990-91, Trenton State; 1989-90, Lock Haven; 1988-89, Trenton State; other past champions include Bloomsburg, Salisbury State and Ithaca.

Assertiveness Pays Off

from Sharon Goldbrenner-Pfluger, Field Hockey and Women's Lacrosse Coach, College of New Jersey

With hundreds of student-athletes striving to attract the attention of college coaches, you must highlight yourself so that a coach becomes familiar with your name and your face. Make contact with coaches at schools in which you are interested during your junior year. Send them a letter, a good resume, a videotape. Then, and this is extremely important, follow up with a phone call a week later. Don't stop there. Follow up with another call in the summer after your junior year and again early in your senior year.

Student-athletes who are a little more assertive are the ones who come out on the high end. Coaches don't forget those who put out that extra effort.

As someone who coaches both field hockey and lacrosse, I definitely think women should try both sports. The basic skills are much the same. Although lacrosse is gaining in popularity, many field hockey players still come to college never having tried it. Then they try it, and it's like a fever. They love it.

For those who worry about balancing sports and classroom work, I find that 95 percent of my players – many of whom play both sports – do better academically during their sports seasons. They just seem to concentrate more.

There are many opportunities for woman athletes today. The most important thing is to take full advantage of them. Because if you don't, those same opportunities may not be available for the next generation of women athletes.

Sharon Goldbrenner-Pfluger has compiled a formidable record at the College of New Jersey (formerly Trenton State), winning six Division III national field hockey championships and eight national lacrosse crowns. In 1990-91, she became the first Division III coach to win national championships in the two sports in the same academic year, a feat her teams repeated in 1991-92 and 1995-96.

FOOTBALL

There is no playoff in NCAA Division IA, with the "national champion" selected by year-end polls of sportswriters by the Associated Press and of college coaches by USA Today.

NCAA Division I-AA champions: 1996-97, Marshall University; 1995-96, Montana; 1994-95, Youngstown State (second straight title, third in four years); 1992-93, Marshall ; 1991-92, Youngstown State; 1990-91 and 1989-90, Georgia Southern (four titles in six years); 1988-89, Furman; other past champions include Northeast Louisiana, Montana State, Southern Illinois, Eastern Kentucky, Idaho State and Boise State.

NCAA Division II champions: 1996-97, Northern Colorado; 1995-96, North Alabama (third title in a row); 1992-93, Jacksonville State; 1991-92, Pittsburg State; 1990-91, North Dakota State (fifth title in eight years); 1989-90, Mississippi College; 1988-89, North Dakota State; other past champions include Troy State, Southwest Texas State, Cal Poly San Luis Obispo, Delaware and Eastern Illinois.

NCAA Division III champions: 1996-97, Mount Union; 1995-95, Wisconsin-La Crosse; 1994-95, Albion; 1993-94, Mount Union; 1992-93, Wisconsin-La Crosse; 1991-92, Ithaca; 1990-91, Allegheny; 1989-90, Dayton; 1988-89, Ithaca; other past champions include Augustana (four in a row from 1983-1986), Wagner, West Georgia, Widener and Baldwin-Wallace.

NAIA Division I champions: 1996-97, Southwestern Oklahoma; 1995-96, Central State (OH); 1994-95, Northeastern State (OK); 1993-94, East Central (OK); 1992-93, Central State; 1991-92, Central Arkansas; 1990-91, Central State; 1989-90 and 1988-89, Carson-Newman.

NAIA Division II champions: 1996-97, Sioux Falls (SD); 1995-96, Findlay (OH) and Central Washington (tie); 1994-95, Westminster (PA); 1993-94, Pacific Lutheran (WA); 1992-93, Findlay; 1991-92, Georgetown (KY); 1990-91, Peru State; 1989-90 and 1988-89, Westminster.

Don't Short-Change Yourself

from Joe Paterno, Head Football Coach, Penn State University

Making a decision on what college or university to attend is one of the critical choices that confronts a young person—athlete or non-athlete.

Playing college sports and getting a quality education is no easy task. It's important the prospective student-athlete understand that in advance. At Penn State, we want our football players to excel on the athletic field. But we also want them to excel in the classroom and to be a part of the mainstream of campus life. If your prospective college doesn't want those things for you, maybe you should take a second look.

In the next four years, you are going to be asked to do some difficult things; to achieve some lofty goals. If you're serious about an education, you are going to have to work at establishing priorities. Plan to enjoy the entire college experience. Learn about art and literature and music and all of the things college has to offer. Don't confine your horizons to the locker room or the gymnasium. College should be a great time. It is the only time a person is really free.

Get to know the coaching staff and gain an appreciation not just for its knowledge of strategy but, every bit as important, the depth of its commitment to education. Does the institution offer academic support? Will academic excellence be expected and encouraged? Can you as an athlete expect to graduate at a rate consistent with the rest of the student body?

I want us to have a winning football team at Penn State because there is no sense being involved in something unless you want to be the best. But we are not going to sacrifice our academic credibility for the sake of a winning team, and you shouldn't either. People often ask me what our best team has been. I tell them I don't know yet. Our best team will be the one that produces the most people who lead active, productive lives in our society.

That should be a goal: A satisfying athletic experience, a meaningful college education and an active, productive life in society. If you settle for anything less, you are short-changing yourself.

Joe Paterno has been on the Penn State football staff more than 40 years and head coach for more than 25. His teams have won two national championships and made more than 20 bowl appearances. The graduation rate of his football players is annually among the tops in the country.

GOLF

Men

NCAA Division I champions: 1996-97, Pepperdine; 1995-96, Arizona State; 1994-95, Oklahoma State; 1993-94, Stanford; 1992-93, Florida; 1991-92, Arizona; 1990-91, Oklahoma State; 1989-90, Arizona; 1988-89, Oklahoma; other past champions include UCLA, Wake Forest, Houston and Brigham Young.

NCAA Division II champions: 1996-97, Columbus State; 1995-96, Florida Southern (eight titles in 15 years); 1993-94, Columbus College (GA); 1992-93, Abilene Christian; 1991-92, Columbus College; 1990-91 and 1989-90, Florida Southern; 1988-89, Columbus; other past champions include Tampa, Troy State and Southwest Texas State.

NCAA Division III champions: 1996-97, Methodist College (NC) (fourth straight title); 1992-93, University of California-San Diego; 1991-92, 1990-91 and 1989-90, Methodist ; 1988-89, Cal State Stanislaus (six titles in a row, 12 in 15 years before moving up to Division II); other past champions include Allegheny, Ramapo and Wooster.

NAIA champions: 1996-97, Mobile; 1995-96, Lynn (FL); 1994-95, Texas Wesleyan; 1993-94, Huntingdon (AL); 1992-93, North Florida; 1991-92, Huntingdon; 1990-91, North Florida; 1989-90, Texas Wesleyan; 1988-89, Guilford (NC).

Women

NCAA Division I champions: 1996-97, Arizona State; 1995-96, Arizona.

NCAA Division II/III champions: 1996-97, Lynn; 1995-96, Methodist College (NC).

NCAA National Collegiate champions (in prior years): 1994-95, Arizona State (third title in a row); 1991-92, San Jose State; 1990-91, UCLA; 1989-90, Arizona State; 1988-89, San Jose State; other past champions include Tulsa, Florida, Miami (FL) and Texas Christian.

NAIA champions: 1996-97, Tri-State (IN); 199596, Lynn (FL) (second straight title); 1993-94, Hardin-Simmonds (TX)

How Good Are You?

from Mike Holder, Men's Golf Coach, Oklahoma State University

Finding a team that matches your golf skills is a lot like finding a college that matches your academic skills. You have to be realistic.

How good are you? And what are your real goals? If you are not being heavily recruited, I'd advise staying close to home. I give in-state students preference, and I think most other coaches do the same.

There is one complication for golfers. If you live in one of the colder parts of the country, you may need to look south where we can play year-round.

How do you catch a coach's eye? Camps and tournaments, especially tournaments, are the places. If you are aiming at a nationally ranked school, then you need to be playing in national tournaments. If you are looking to a school in your state, then state tournaments are the ticket.

A lot of people are sending videos these days. But you better have something to back them up. If you can't show some low scores or high finishes in tournaments, then it doesn't matter what you look like on a video.

It is very important for you to find a program that offers you an opportunity to make the team. You will not improve if you do not get some tournament experience. A lot of great players have developed at smaller schools because they were given the opportunity to compete on a regular basis in tournaments.

Mike Holder's Oklahoma State Cowboys have been NCAA Division I national champions seven times — in 1995, 1991, 1987, 1983, 1980, 1978, and 1976 — and runners-up seven times. Players such as Bob Tway and Scott Verplank have gone on to the PGA tour.

ICE HOCKEY

NCAA Division I champions: 1996-97, North Dakota; 1995-96, Michigan; 1994-95, Boston University; 1993-94, Lake Superior State; 1992-93, Maine; 1991-92, Lake Superior State; 1990-91, Northern Michigan; 1989-90, University of Wisconsin; 1988-89, Harvard; other past winners include North Dakota, Michigan State, Rensselaer, Bowling Green and Minnesota.

Division II champions: 1996-97, Bemidji State; 1995-96, Alabama-Huntsville; 1994-95, Bemidji State (fourth title in a row). (Championship suspended after the 1984 season and reinstated in 1992-93.)

Division III champions: 1996-97, Middlebury (third straight title); 1993-94, University of Wisconsin-River Falls; 1992-93, University of Wisconsin-Stevens Point; 1991-92, Plattsburgh State; 1990-91, 1989-90 and 1988-89, University of Wisconsin-Stevens Point; other past champions, Bemidji State, Rochester Institute of Technology and Babson College.

Junior Leagues Attract the Attention

from Mark Mazzoleni, Hockey Coach, Miami University (Ohio)

One of the best ways to get the attention of college coaches is by playing Tier 2 junior hockey. Both the U.S. Junior Hockey League and the North American Junior Hockey League are closely scouted by coaches. You can play until you're 20, so many of the players have finished high school and are looking for the right college. The first priority of the junior leagues is to put kids into school.

For kids from parts of the country not known for hockey, the juniors offer a chance to show how good they are. You might score 100 goals and not get any notice if a coach knows the competition is weak. But players from hockey hotbeds can profit, too, from the increased competition of the juniors. They play 45-50 games a year, many more than high schools are permitted to play.

Another avenue is prep schools. Many of them have excellent hockey programs and they are geared to serve as feeders for Division III colleges in the East.

Above all, don't neglect the academics. It takes more than athletic skill to get into college. Your high school grades are important and you should take the entrance tests as many times as you can. Make personal contact with the schools in which you are interested to be sure you are taking the right high school courses and the right test – the ACT is favored in the Midwest, the SATs in the East. Entrance requirements are getting tougher all the time and it is up to you to be prepared.

Mark Mazzoleni moved on to Division I, first as an assistant at Minnesota and then as head coach at Miami of Ohio, after coaching the University of Wisconsin-Stevens Point to three straight NCAA Division III national championships.

LACROSSE

Women

NCAA National Collegiate champions: 1996-97, Maryland (third straight title); 1993-94, Princeton; 1992-93, Virginia; 1991-92, Maryland; 1990-91, Virginia; 1989-90, Harvard; 1988-89, Penn State; other past champions include Temple, New Hampshire, Delaware and Massachusetts.

NCAA Division III champions: 1996-97, Middlebury; 1995-96, College of New Jersey (formerly Trenton State, fourth straight title, seventh since 1985); 1989-90 and 1988-89, Ursinus.

Men

NCAA Division I champions: 1996-97, Princeton (second straight title); 1994-95, Syracuse; 1993-94, Princeton; 1992-93, Syracuse; 1991-92, Princeton; 1990-91, North Carolina; 1989-90, Syracuse (third title in a row); other past champions include Johns Hopkins (seven times), Cornell, Maryland and Virginia.

NCAA Division II champions: 1996-97, New York Tech; 1995-96, Long Island-C.W. Post; 1994-95, Adelphi (NY); 1993-94, Springfield (MA); 1992-93, Adelphi. (Championship was suspended after the 1981 season, reinstated in 1993.)

NCAA Division III champions: 1996-97, Nazareth (second straight title); 1994-95, Salisbury State (MD) (second title in a row); 1992-93, Hobart (13th title in 14 years); 1991-92, Nazareth. Other top teams include Ohio Wesleyan, Washington (MD), Roanoke and Cortland State.

Don't Sit Around and Wait

from Dave Urick, Men's Lacrosse Coach, Georgetown University

The college selection process for a prospective student-athlete is by no means an exact science. This makes establishing and maintaining meaningful communication with the coaches at schools in which you are interested very important.

Do not sit around and wait for something to happen. College visits, admission interviews and the application process should be well planned and organized. Work with the coach, but do not expect him or her to hand-walk you through the process.

Be sure, as best you can, to match your potential ability with the academic and athletic competitiveness of the schools you are seriously considering.

Finally, and perhaps most importantly, if you will need financial assistance to attend college, familiarize yourself and your parents with the proper procedures. Promptness is a key. Good luck!

Dave Urick's Hobart College teams won 10 Division III national championships in a row. He moved to Division I Georgetown in 1989.

SKIING

Men and Women

NCAA National Collegiate champions: 1996-97, Utah (second straight title); 1994-95, Colorado (11th title since 1970, 13th in all); 1993-94, Vermont; 1992-93, Utah (four titles between 1984 and 1988, eight overall); 1991-92, Vermont; 1990-91, Colorado; 1989-90 and 1988-89, Vermont; other past champions include Denver (14 titles in all, the last one in 1971), Wyoming and Dartmouth.

A Point Profile Is a Must

from Richard Rokos, Ski Coach, University of Colorado

Recruiting skiers is at such a high level these days, internationally as well as nationally, that a high school skier must have a low point profile to even be considered for a scholarship.

You get a point profile by joining the United States Ski Association (the AFSI is the international equivalent) and participating in its meets. The earlier the better, because it takes a while to develop the kind of profile that college coaches pay attention to.

Every skier starts with 990 points and the goal is to get down as low as you can. A very talented skier should be down to 300 points the first year and to 100 the second. But from then on it gets very tough. The formula is very complicated, but the lower you get the harder it is to cut your numbers. Right now, the top colleges are looking for skiers whose profile is in the low teens.

Skiers who can't show the numbers needed to draw scholarship attention do have another approach. They can use a club team as a starting point to make the varsity. Here at Colorado we have more than 200 skiers involved on the club teams and developmental teams. Almost every year we have someone make it to the varsity from the club teams. These are usually skiers who didn't have impressive profile numbers, and who we hadn't seen. They used the club teams to show their abilities and work ethic.

Most colleges in snow country have club teams even if they don't have varsities. They offer wonderful competition for those who don't ski at the national or international level.

Richard Rokos' ski team have won NCAA national collegiate championships in 1994-95 and 1990-91.

SOCCER

Men

NCAA Division I champions: 1996-97, St. John's (NY); 1995-96, Wisconsin; 1994-95, Virginia (fourth straight title); 1990-91, UCLA; 1989-90, Virginia and Santa Clara (tie); 1988-89, Indiana (also won back-to-back titles in 1982 and 1983); other past champions include Clemson, Duke, Connecticut, San Francisco and SIU-Edwardsville.

NCAA Division II champions: 1996-97, Grand Canyon; 1995-96, Southern Connecticut State; 1994-95, Tampa; 1993-95, Seattle Pacific; 1992-93, Southern Connecticut State; 1991-92, Florida Tech; 1990-91, Southern Connecticut State; 1989-90, New Hampshire College; 1988-89, Florida Tech; other past champions include Florida International, Tampa, Lock Haven and Alabama A&M.

NCAA Division III champions: 1996-97, College of New Jersey (formerly Trenton State); 1995-96, Williams; 1994-95, Bethany (WV); 1993-94, University of California-San Diego; 1992-93, Kean College; 1991-92, UC-San Diego; 1990-91, Glassboro State; 1989-90, Elizabethtown; 1988-89, UC-San Diego; other past champions include North Carolina-Greensboro (five titles between 1982 and 1987), Wheaton, Babson and Lock Haven.

NAIA champions: 1996-97, Lindsey Wilson (KY) (second straight title); 1994-95, West Virginia Wesleyan; 1993-94, Sangamon State (now University of Illinois at Springfleld.);1992-93, Belhaven (MS); 1991-92, Lynn (FL); 1990-91 and 1989-90, West Virginia Wesleyan; 1988-89, Sangamon State.

Women

NCAA Division I champions: 1996-97, North Carolina (13th title in tournament's 16 years); 1995-96, Notre Dame; 1994-95, North Carolina (ninth title in a row); George Mason (VA) was champion in 1985-86.

NCAA Division II champions: 1996-97, Franklin Pierce (third straight title); 1993-94, 1992-93 and 1991-92, Barry University; 1990-91, Sonoma State; 1989-90, Barry; 1988-89, Cal State Hayward (first year for playoffs.)

NCAA Division III champions: 1996-97, UC San Diego (second straight title); 1995-95, Trenton State (second title in a row); 1992-93, Cortland State; 1991-92 and 1990-91, Ithaca; 1989-90, UC-San Diego; 1988-89, William Smith; other past champion, Rochester (1986 and 1987).

NAIA champions: 1996-97, Simon Fraser (BC); 1995-96, Lynn (FL) (second title in a row); 1993-94, Berry (GA); 1992-93, Lynn; 1991-92, Pacific Lutheran; 1990-91, Berry; 1989-90 and 1988-89, Pacific Lutheran.

Beware of Being Oversold

from Jerry Yeagley, Men's Soccer Coach, Indiana University

Your high school coach is an important player in your search for the right college. But sometimes coaches oversell a student-athlete's abilities. You may be the best player on your team and the coach–especially a volunteer or someone not familiar with the college scene–gets carried away.

How can you be sure you are getting a realistic appraisal of your talent? Here are some suggestions:

- Watch college teams in which you are interested play–not once, but several times. Do you feel comfortable with the level of skills you see there? That's a very important sign.
- Attend a summer camp where your abilities will be evaluated by college coaches. If you have your heart set on a particular school, by all means attend its camp. On our IU team, 11 of the 18 varsity players attended our summer camp. This should be the summer after your sophomore year at the very latest. Our top player at IU first came to camp when he was 12.
- Try out for the best select soccer team you can. This can provide a good guide for you. If you don't make the team, then you may need to adjust your sights a bit lower. If you do, remember that college coaches follow the top select teams closely. A recommendation from a coach of one of these teams can make a real difference.

One other very important point: Before writing to a college coach, take the time to learn all you can about the coach and the program; how successful it is, how competitive. Your letter should show that this is a college you really want to attend and not just one of a score you are sending form letters to. A "Dear Coach" (no name) letter won't get you anywhere.

Jerry Yeagley's Hoosier soccer team won NCAA Division I national championships in 1988, 1983 and 1982. He has been named to the U.S. Soccer Federation's Hall of Fame.

SOFTBALL

NCAA Division I champions: 1996-97, Arizona (second straight title); 1994-95, UCLA (eighth title in 13 years); 1993-94 and 1992-93, Arizona; 1991-92, UCLA; 1990-91, Arizona; 1989-90, UCLA (third title in a row); other past champions include Texas A&M and Cal State Fullerton.

NCAA Division II champions: 1996-97, California (PA); 1995-96, Kennesaw State (second straight title); 1993-94, Merrimack (MA); 1992-93, Florida Southern; 1991-92, Missouri Southern; 1990-91, Augustana; 1989-90, Cal State Bakersfield (third title in a row); other past champions include Cal State Northridge (four titles between 1983 and 1987), Stephen F. Austin State and Sam Houston State.

NCAA Division III champions: 1996-97, Simpson; 1995-96, Trenton State (now College of New Jersey); 1994-95, Chapman (CA); 1993-94, Trenton State; 1992-93, Central College (IA); 1991-92, Trenton State; 1990-91 and 1989-90, Eastern Connecticut State; 1988-89, Trenton State; other past champions include Buena Vista.

NAIA champions: 1996-97, Oklahoma City (fourth title in a row); 1992-93, West Florida; 1991-92, Pacific Lutheran; 1990-91, Hawaii-Loa; 1989-90, Kearney State (NE); 1988-89, Saginaw Valley.

Some Things You Can Do

from Susan Craig, Softball Coach, University of New Mexico

Finding the right college and/or an athletic scholarship is a real challenge. Here are some tips that may make things easier. Start early. We like to watch athletes compete for a couple of years to get a good evaluation of their skills. Also, it's best to take the SAT or ACT tests more than once to get the best possible score.

Compete. Play at the highest level available. Also attend as many college camps or instructional schools as you can.

Educate yourself about the sport. Read everything available on your sport or position. Watch older youth teams or college games so you can see what skills are needed to play at that level. Keep up with the NCAA rankings. Write the sports information offices of colleges in which you are interested and ask for brochures, schedules and information on the teams' records and awards.

Get to know the coach. Talk to several former athletes, not just one. Talk to other coaches who deal regularly with that coach—one of your area youth coaches, for example. Visit the campus and watch the team practice and play. Learn all you can about the program's philosophy. Do they like to steal bases, hit and run, what do they do with runners at first and third?

Leaving or staying. Leaving home and being on your own is part of the growing-up process. But some athletes cannot deal with that and are better off attending a school close to home. Also, don't forget about the weather. There are good softball programs in all parts of the country, but you'll have more chances to play if you choose a college in one of the warmer areas.

Susan Craig started the successful University of New Mexico softball program 16 years ago. Considered one of the top teachers in the game, she is the author—with her co-head coach Ken Johnson—of The Softball Handbook.

SWIMMING AND DIVING

Women

NCAA Division I champions: 1996-97, Southern California; 1995-96, Stanford (fifth title in a row); 1990-91 and 1989-90, Texas (seven titles in eight years); 1988-89, Stanford; other champion, Florida (1982).

NCAA Division II champions: 1996-97, Drury; 1995-96, Air Force Academy (second straight title); 1993-94, Oakland (fifth straight title); 1988-89, Cal State Northridge (third title in a row); other champions include Clarion and South Florida.

NCAA Division III champions: 1996-97, Kenyon (14th title in a row); only other champion, Williams (1981-82 and 1982-83).

NAIA champions: 1996-97, Simon Fraser (BC); 1995-96, Puget Sound (WA); 1994-95, Simon Fraser; 1993-94, Drury (MO) (Third title in a row); 1990-91, Simon Fraser; 1989-90 and 1988-89, Puget Sound.

Men

NCAA Division I champions: 1996-97, Auburn; 1995-96, Texas; 1994-95, Michigan; 1993-94, Stanford (third straight title); 1990-91, Texas (fourth title in a row); other past champions include Florida, UCLA, California, Tennessee, Southern California and Indiana.

NCAA Division II champions: 1996-97, Oakland (fourth title in a row); 1992-93, Cal State Bakersfield (eighth title in a row); other champions include Cal State Northridge (nine titles between 1975 and 1985) and Cal State Chico.

NCAA Division III champions: 1996-97, Kenyon (18th title in a row). Only other champions are Johns Hopkins (three titles between 1977 and 1979), St. Lawrence and Cal State Chico.

NAIA champions: 1996-97, Puget Sound (WA) (Third straight title); 1993-94, Drury (MO) (sixth title in a row).

Keep an Open Mind

from Jim Steen, Swimming Coach, Kenyon College

Keeping an open mind is very important in choosing a college and a sports program. I see too many students who come to visit with a prejudice either for or against a school. One is as bad as the other.

Be an inquiring sort of person, but one who is receptive to being surprised or enlightened by what you see. Ask questions—of coaches, faculty, admissions people, students. And listen carefully to their answers.

Before you visit a school, you should have some idea that you would match up there both scholastically and athletically. Start with a personal letter—not a form letter—to the coach. Then check out all the information you receive and decide if you and the college could be a fit.

If the answer is yes, arrange a visit with the coach. If you are unsure about anything, ask. But you also must ask yourself what would satisfy you. Do you need just to be on a team or would you be happier somewhere else where you could be a starter? Get a direct commitment from the coach whenever possible about just what your role may be.

As you go through the selection process, you should narrow your focus to no more than four schools—three top choices and a backup. That's about all any person can give careful consideration to. And don't wait until the last minute to do the paperwork, especially the financial aid forms. Complete those even if you are not sure you are going to qualify.

As a coach, I play at most an indirect role in helping swimmers get into Kenyon. My real role is helping students decide if this is the place they really want and if they qualify. I want athletes to know they got in on their own merits.

Jim Steen's Kenyon swimmers have won an unprecedented 18 NCAA Division III men's national championships in a row as well as 14 consecutive women's championships.

TENNIS

Women

NCAA Division I champions: 1996-97, Stanford; 1995-96, Florida; 1994-95, Texas; 1993-94, Georgia; 1992-93, Texas; 1991-92, Florida; 1990-91, Stanford (sixth title in a row and eighth since 1982); Southern Cal won titles in 1983 and 1985; other top teams include UCLA, Miami (FL) and Trinity (TX).

NCAA Division II champions: 1996-97, Lynn; 1995-96, Armstrong State (GA) (Second straight title); 1993-94, North Florida; 1992-93, University of California-Davis; 1991-92 and 1990-91, Cal Poly Pomona; 1989-90, UC Davis; 1988-89, SIU-Edwardsville (fourth title in a row); other past champions are Tennessee-Chattanooga and Cal State Northridge.

NCAA Division III champions: 1996-97, Kenyon; 1995-96, Emory; 1994-95, Kenyon; 1993-94, UC San Diego; 1992-93, Kenyon; 1991-92, Pomona-Pitzer; 1990-91, Mary Washington; 1989-90, Gustavus Adolphus; 1988-89, UC San Diego; other past champions include Trenton State (now College of New Jersey), Davidson, Principia and Occidental.

NAIA champions: 1996-97, BYU-Hawaii; 1995-96, Lynn (FL) (Second straight title); 1993-94, Mobile; 1992-93, Lynn; 1991-92, Auburn-Montgomery (AL); 1990-91, Flagler (FL), (third title in a row).

Men

NCAA Division I champions: 1996-97, Stanford (third title in a row and 15th since 1973); 1993-94 and 1992-93, Southern California; 1991-92, Stanford; 1990-91, Southern California; 1989-90, Stanford (third title in a row); other past champions include Georgia and UCLA.

NCAA Division II champions: 1996-97, Lander College (SC) (fifth title in a row); 1991-92, UC-Davis; 1990-91, Rollins; 1989-90, Cal Poly San Luis Obispo; 1988-89, Hampton; other past champions include Chapman, SIU-Edwardsville and UC-Irvine.

NCAA Division III champions: 1996-97, Washington (MD); 1995-96, UC-Santa Cruz (second straight title); 1993-94, Washington (MD); 1992-93, Kalamazoo (third title in a row); 1989-90, Swarthmore; 1988-89, UC-Santa Cruz; other past champions include Washington and Lee, Redlands and Gustavus Adolphus.

NAIA champions: 1996-97, Mobile; 1995-96, Auburn-Montgomery (AL) (Second straight title); 1993-94, Texas-Tyler; 1992-93, Mobile; 1991-92 and 1990-91, Lander (SC); 1989-90, Elon (NC); 1988-89, Texas-Tyler.

Get Some Tournament Experience

from Bob Meyers, Former Women's Tennis Coach, Southern Illinois University-Edwardsville

If you hope to play tennis on a college team – especially at a Division I or Division II school – you need to get all the experience you can. And that doesn't mean just in high school matches.

Play in as many tournaments as you possibly can – at the highest level you can qualify for. This will get you a United States Tennis Association ranking and that's something that means a lot to college coaches. They are are looking for mature players with a lot of experience. And the rankings help them pick and choose. As a Division II coach, I looked for players ranked No. 70 or above on a national scale. Other schools have their own standards.

I received letters from hundreds of tennis players who were interested in my team. Unfortunately, most of those letters didn't tell me much about the player's skill level. If you are sending an athletic resume to a coach, be as specific as possible. Tell him or her what tournaments you have played in, who you played against and the scores. The coach may know nothing about you, but he or she may recognize your opponent's name. Even a loss in a close match says something about your game. The more you can tell a coach about your skills the better chance you will have.

For good high school players who are not ranked and who aren't being recruited by a Division I or II school, the best choice may well be a Division III college. That means no athletic scholarship, but other financial aid may amount to just about as much. A player who blossoms in Division III can always transfer to a higher-ranked school.

Of course, you can always be a walk-on and try to make a team that hasn't recruited you. But you have to realize you'll be up against players with a lot of experience. College sports should be fun, not something that overwhelms you. Picking the proper level at which to play can make it both competitive and fun.

Bob Meyers' Southern Illinois University-Edwardsville teams won four straight NCAA Division II national women's titles from 1986 to 1989. He retired from coaching after the 1989 season.

TRACK AND FIELD/CROSS COUNTRY

Cross Country

Men

NCAA Division I champions: 1996-97, Stanford; 1995-96, Arkansas (eighth title in last 12 years); 1994-95, Iowa State; 1993-94, Arkansas (fourth title in a row); 1989-90, Iowa State; 1988-89, Wisconsin; other past champions include University of Texas-El Paso, Oregon and Tennessee.

NCAA Division II champions: 1996-97, South Dakota State; 1995-96, Western State; 1994-95, Adams State (CO) (third straight title); 1991-92, Massachusetts-Lowell; 1990-91, Edinboro; 1989-90, South Dakota State; 1988-89, Edinboro and Mankato State (tie); other past champions include Southeast Missouri State, Cal Poly Pomona, Eastern Washington, Millersville and Humboldt State.

NCAA Division III champions: 1996-97, Wisconsin-La Crosse; 1995-96, Williams (second straight title); 1993-94 and 1992-93, North Central; 1991-92, Rochester; 1990-91, 1989-90 and 1988-89 University of Wisconsin-Oshkosh; other past champions include St. Thomas (MN), Luther and Brandeis.

NAIA champions: 1996-97, Lubbock Christian (seventh title in a row); 1989-90 and 1988-89, Adams State.

Women

NCAA Division I champions: 1996-97, Stanford; 1995-96, Providence; 1994-95, Villanova (sixth title in a row); 1988-89, Kentucky; other past champions include Oregon, Texas, Wisconsin and Virginia.

NCAA Division II champions: 1996-97, Adams State (fifth straight title); 1991-92, Cal Poly San Luis Obispo (10th title in a row); only other champion is South Dakota State (1981).

NCAA Division III champions: 1996-97, Wisconsin-Oshkosh; 1995-96, Cortland State (fourth title in a row); 1991-92, Wisconsin-Oshkosh; 1990-91 and 1989-90, Cortland State; 1988-89, University of Wisconsin-Oshkosh; other champions include St. Thomas (MN), Franklin and Marshall, Wisconsin-La Crosse and Central (IA).

NAIA champions: 1996-97, Simon Fraser (BC); 1995-96, Puget Sound (fourth straight title); 1991-92, Adams State; 1990-91, Western State; 1989-90, Adams State; 1988-89, Pacific Lutheran.

Track and Field

Women's Indoor

NCAA Division I champions: 1996-97, Louisiana State (fifth straight title); 1991-92, Florida; 1990-91, Louisiana State; 1989-90, Texas; 1988-89, Louisiana State; other past champions include Florida State and Nebraska.

NCAA Division II champions: 1996-97, Abilene Christian (fifth straight title, eighth in 11 years); 1991-92, Alabama A&M; 1990-91, Abilene Christian; St. Augustine's has won two titles.

NCAA Division III champions: 1996-97, Christopher Newport; 1995-96, Wisconsin-Oshkosh (third title in a row); 1992-93, Lincoln University (PA); 1991-92, Christopher Newport; 1990-91, Cortland State; 1989-90, 1988-89 and 1987-88, Christopher Newport. University of Massachusetts-Boston also won three in a row (1985-87).

NAIA champions: 1996-97, Southern-New Orleans; 1995-96, Central State (OH); 1994-95, Southern-New Orleans; 1993-94, Wayland Baptist (TX); 1992-93, Central State; 1991-92, Simon Fraser (BC); 1990-91, Prairie View; 1989-90, Simon Fraser; 1988-89, Midland Lutheran.

Men's Indoor

NCAA Division I champions: 1996-97, Arkansas; 1995-96, George Mason; 1994-95, Arkansas (12th title in a row); other past champions include Southern Methodist, University of Texas-El Paso, Villanova and Washington State.

NCAA Division II champions: 1996-97, Abilene Christian (second straight title) ; 1994-95, St. Augustine; 1993-94 and 1992-93, Abilene Christian; 1991-92, St. Augustine (sixth title in a row); Abilene Christian tied for the title in 1987-88 and Southeast Missouri State won in 1984-85.

NCAA Division III champions: 1996-97, Wisconsin-La Crosse; 1995-96, Lincoln (PA) (second straight title); 1993-94, Wisconsin-La Crosse (fourth title in a row); 1989-90, Lincoln (PA); 1988-89, North Central. Other past champions were Frostburg State and St. Thomas (MN).

NAIA champions: 1996-97, Life (GA); 1995-96, Azusa Pacific (CA); 1994-95, Lubbock Christian (TX); 1993-94 and 1992-93, Central State (OH); 1991-92, Adams State (CO); 1990-91, Lubbock Christian; 1989-90, Adams State; 1988-89, Wayland Baptist.

Women's Outdoor

NCAA Division I champions: 1996-97, Louisiana State (11th title in a row); other past champions include Texas, Oregon, Florida State and UCLA.

NCAA Division II champions: 1996-97, St. Augustine's; 1995-96, Abilene Christian (second straight title); 1993-94, Alabama A&M (third title in a row); 1990-91, Cal Poly San Luis Obispo (third title in a row). Abilene Christian won four straight titles from 1985 to 1988.

NCAA Division III champions: 1996-97, Wisconsin-Oshkosh (third straight title); 1993-94, Christopher Newport; 1992-93, Lincoln (PA); 1991-92, Christopher Newport; 1990-91 and 1989-90, Wisconsin-Oshkosh; 1988-89, Christopher Newport (third title in a row). Other past champions include University of Massachusetts-Boston, Cortland State, Wisconsin-La Crosse and Central (IA).

NAIA champions: 1996-97, Southern-New Orleans; 1995-96, Central State (OH); 1994-95, Southern-New Orleans; 1993-94, Central State (fourth title in a row); 1989-90 and 1988-89, Prairie View (TX).

Men's Outdoor

NCAA Division I champions: 199697, Arkansas (sixth straight title); 1990-91, Tennessee; 1989-90 and 1988-89, Louisiana State. Other past champions include UCLA, Southern Methodist, Southern Cal, Oregon and University of Texas-El Paso.

NCAA Division II champions: 1996-97, Abilene Christian (second straight title; also won seven straight between 1982 and 1988); 1994-95, St. Augustine (seventh title in a row); other past champions include Cal Poly San Luis Obispo, Cal State Los Angeles and Cal State Hayward.

NCAA Division III champions: 1996-97, Wisconsin-La Crosse; 1995-96, Lincoln (PA) (Second straight title); 1993-94, North Central; 1992-93, Wisconsin-La Crosse (third title in a row); 1989-90, Lincoln (PA); 1988-89, North Central; other past champions include Frostburg State, Glassboro State (five straight titles between 1980 and 1984) and Slippery Rock.

NAIA champions: 1996-97, Life (GA); 1995-96, Lubbbock Christian (TX); 1994-95 and 1993-94, Azusa Pacific (CA); 1992-93, Central State (OH); 1991-92 and 1990-91, Azusa Pacific; 1989-90, Oklahoma Baptist; 1988-89, Azusa Pacific.

Explore All the Possibilities

from Wes Kittley, Head Track Coach, Abilene Christian University

I am constantly surprised at the amount of financial aid available to students — and that doesn't mean just student-athletes.

The aid is there; you just have to look for it. As a Division II coach, the athletic scholarships I can give are limited. Many of the young athletes I recruit will get no athletic scholarships at all. That's where the other possibilities come in.

Visit the campus with your parents and talk to the financial aid office. Have family income figures ready. You will probably be pleasantly surprised. There are academic scholarships, ethnic and other special scholarships, Pell Grants, state grants, matching grants and many more. You may well come up with a package that goes a long way toward paying the cost of your college education. Start looking at what is available during your junior year in high school for best results.

As a track coach, I have an advantage over coaches in some other sports. I get periodic reports on the best times and distances in many states. Yet there are many borderline athletes who could help my team that I never hear about. By all means, write the coaches at schools you are interested in and let them know about you — not just your sports skills, either, but about you as a student and as a person.

Videotapes can be useful, too, but keep them short. If the school you have your eye on has a summer camp, that's a good place to catch the coach's eye.

It is getting harder and harder for smaller schools to get the real blue-chip athletes. But we all need good student-athletes and that could be you. So let us coaches know you are out there.

Wes Kittley's women's track team has won five straight national Division II women's indoor titles and eight in the last 11 years, as well as outdoor crowns in 1994-95 and 1995-96 and a four-year stretch from 1985 through 1988. He moved up from women's coach to head coach for the 1993-94 season. Since then, his men's teams have won three Division II indoor crowns and two outdoor championships.

VOLLEYBALL

Women

NCAA Division I champions: 1996-97, Stanford; 1995-96, Nebraska; 1994-95, Stanford; 1993-94, Long Beach State; 1992-93, Stanford; 1991-92 and 1990-91, UCLA; 1989-90, Long Beach State; 1988-89, Texas; other past champions include Hawaii, Pacific and Southern Cal.

NCAA Division II champions: 1996-97, Nebraska-Omaha; 1995-96, Barry; 1994-95 and 1993-94, Northern Michigan; 1992-93, Portland State (fourth title in last 10 years); 1991-92 and 1990-91, West Texas State; 1989-90, Cal State Bakersfield; 1988-89, Portland State; other past champions include Cal State Northridge, UC-Riverside and Cal State Sacramento.

NCAA Division III champions: 1996-97, Washington University (MO) (sixth title in a row); 1990-91, UC-San Diego (fourth title in five years); 1989-90, Washington University; other past champions are Elmhurst and La Verne.

NAIA champions: 1996-97, Brigham Young-Hawaii (third straight title); 1993-94, Puget Sound (WA); 1992-93 and 1991-92, Brigham Young-Hawaii; 1990-91, Hawaii Pacific; 1989-90, Fresno Pacific; 1988-89, Hawaii-Hilo.

Men

NCAA National Collegiate champions: 1996-97, Stanford; 1995-96, UCLA (second straight tile and 16th in 25 years); 1993-94, Penn State; 1992-93, UCLA; 1991-92, Pepperdine (fourth title); 1990-91, Long Beach State; 1989-90, Southern Cal (fourth title); 1988-89, UCLA; other past champion is San Diego State.

Don't Let Size Scare You Away

from Mick Haley, Head Coach, USA Women's National Volleyball Team

High school kids do some crazy things in the process of picking a college. One is to let the size of a school scare them off without ever finding out how that size can work in their favor.

Major athletic programs—the good ones—have tremendous resources. Many provide academic coaches, study halls, counseling programs. Still, some students will choose a small school without understanding that its athletic program may be on a shoestring budget, and they will be left to work out their own problems.

Large size is no guarantee, however. Athletes, especially women, should ask some tough questions about the kind of support they can expect. For example:

• What percentage of student-athletes graduate? I would find it scary if the figure for all athletes is not in the 60th percentile. What percent of athletes who complete their eligibility graduate? That figure should be in the 90s.

- What is the GPA of the team? What are their majors? If they are all in PE, are they being guided that way?
- Is there a study hall program? Can you get help in how to study? Are tutors available? Enough tutors? Who pays for them?
- Is there a rehabilitation department to help you come back from an injury? How does the school handle career-ending injury? Is there a nutrition program, and does the school require you to establish a certain weight? Is there drug education? An independent counseling program, and is it aimed at help you or helping the team?

It is vitally important that you watch games and practices to check out the coach's style. Some athletes do their best when being screamed at. Others don't. Some high school kids seem to have a self-destructive streak in picking a coaching style that is totally wrong for them. Don't you make the same mistake!

Mick Haley became head coach of the USA Women's National Volleyball Team in 1996. Before that, he was head coach at the University of Texas, where his team won the 1988-89 NCAA Division I championship, the first team outside of California or Hawaii to take a national volleyball crown.

OTHER SPORTS

Fencing

Men and Women

NCAA national champions: 1996-97, Penn State (third straight title); 1993-94, Notre Dame; 1992-93 and 1991-92, Columbia/Columbia-Barnard; 1990-91 and 1989-90, Penn State. (Changed to a combined sport after the 1989 season.)

Women

NCAA national champions: 1988-89, Wayne State (second straight title); other past champions include Notre Dame, Pennsylvania and Yale.

Men

NCAA national champions: 1988-89, Columbia (third straight title); other past champions include Notre Dame, Wayne State, Pennsylvania and New York University.

Gymnastics

Women

NCAA national champions: 1996-97, UCLA; 1995-96, Alabama; 1994-95, Utah (second straight title, ninth since 1982);1992-93, Georgia; 1991-92, Utah; 1990-91, Alabama (also won in 1987-88); 1989-90, Utah; 1988-89, Georgia.

Men

NCAA national champions: 1996-97, California; 1995-96, Ohio State; 1994-95, Stanford; 1993-94, Nebraska (eighth title); 1992-93 and 1991-92, Stanford; 1990-91, Oklahoma; 1989-90, Nebraska; 1988-89, Illinois (ninth title, but first since 1958); other past champions include Penn State (nine titles), UCLA, Arizona State, Ohio State, Indiana State, California, Iowa State and Southern Illinois.

Rifle

Men and women

NCAA national champions: 1996-97, West Virginia (ninth title in 10 years and 12th since 1983); 1993-94, Alaska-Fairbanks; other past champions are Murray State and Tennessee Tech.

Water Polo

NCAA national champions: 1995-96, UCLA; 1994-95 and 1993-94, Stanford; 1992-93, California (fifth title in six years, 11th in all); 1989-90, UC-Irvine.

Wrestling

NCAA Division I champions: 1996-97, Iowa (sixth title in seven years, 15th title since 1975, including nine in a row between 1978 and 1986); 1993-94, Oklahoma State (19th title overall); 1989-90 and 1988-89 Oklahoma State; other past champions include Arizona State, Iowa State and Oklahoma.

NCAA Division II champions: 1996-97, San Francisco State; 1995-96. Pittsburgh-Johnstown; 1994-95, Central Oklahoma (fourth straight title); 1990-91, Nebraska-Omaha; 1989-90 and 1988-89, Portland State; other past champions include North Dakota State, SIU-Edwardsville, Cal State Bakersfield, Northern Iowa and Cal Poly San Luis Obispo.

NCAA Division III champions: 1996-97, Augsburg (MN); 1995-96, Wartburg; 1994-95, Augsburg (third title in six years); 1993-94, Ithaca; 1992-93, Augsburg ; 1991-92, Brockport State; 1990-91, Augsburg; 1989-90 and 1988-89, Ithaca; other past champions include St. Lawrence, Trenton State and Montclair State.

NAIA champions: 1996-97, Missouri Valley (second straight title); 1994-95, Findlay (OH); 1993-94, Southern Oregon and Western Montana (tie); 1992-93, Simon Fraser; 1991-92 and 1990-91, Northern Montana; 1989-90, Adams State; 1988-89, Central State (OK).

Section III

NCAA, Division I-A

These are the big football schools – I-A being a football-only classification. They are the ones you see on TV on Saturday afternoons and in the bowl games. There is no NCAA playoff in this division, the "national champion" being crowned on the basis of year-end rankings in the Associated Press poll of sportswriters and the *USA Today* poll of college coaches. The NCAA requires that Division I-A schools have stadiums that seat at least 30,000, and home attendance must average 17,000. Division I-A schools must offer seven varsity sports for men or mixed teams and seven for women (or six for men or mixed teams and eight for women). All offer football scholarships, with the exception of the service academies (there is no information from them in most of the chart categories because of this).

An **n/a** on the chart denotes missing information, in most cases because no freshmen athletes were recruited in some sport in 1990-91.

The information listed here is from the 1997 NCAA Division I Graduation-Rates Report, copies of which have been sent to all high school guidance departments. The report contains additional information that you may wish to examine.

Percentage Graduating by 1994

	'90 freshman	'90 freshman athletes	male athletes	female athletes	'90 football recruits	'90 basketball recruits
ALABAMA						
Auburn University Auburn, Ala. 36849 (334) 844-9891	66	55	48	72	43	0
University of Alabama Tuscaloosa, Ala. 35487 (205) 348-3697	57	59	51	70	44	0
ARIZONA						
Arizona State University Tempe, Ariz. 85287 (602) 965-6360	46	53	44	75	39	20
University of Arizona Tucson, Ariz. 85721 (602) 621-2200	51	64	56	79	65	0
ARKANSAS						
University of Arkansas Fayetteville, Ark. 72701 (501) 575-2755	41	34	21	63	18	25

	'90 freshman	'90 freshman athletes	Percentage Graduating by 1994 male athletes	female athletes	'90 football recruits	'90 basketball recruits
Arkansas State University State University, Ark. 72467 (501) 972-3030	31	49	47	56	40	0
CALIFORNIA						
California State University Fresno, Calif. 93740 (209) 278-3178	47	38	33	50	35	0
San Diego State University San Diego, Calif. 92182 (619) 594-3019	34	40	34	60	29	0
San Jose State University San Jose, Calif. 95192 (408) 924-1200	39	46	46	46	100	100
Stanford University Stanford, Calif. 94305 (415) 723-4596	94	91	95	80	94	100
University of California Berkeley, Calif. 94720 (510) 642-5316	80	64	52	82	44	33
University of California Los Angeles, Calif. 90095 (310) 206-6382	77	57	52	68	63	67
University of the Pacific Stockton, Calif. 95211 (209) 946-2248	59	70	60	82	83	33
Univ. of Southern California Los Angeles, Calif. 90089 (213) 740-8177	67	57	49	75	59	33
COLORADO						
Colorado State University Fort Collins, Colo. 80523 (970) 491-5300	56	33	30	39	37	50
University of Colorado Boulder, Colo. 80309 (303) 492-7931	66	51	56	40	53	0
U.S. Air Force Academy USAF Academy, Colo. 80840 (719) 472-4008	77	—	—	—	—	—

	Percentage Graduating by 1994				
	'90 freshman	'90 freshman athletes	male athletes	female athletes	'90 football recruits	'90 basketball recruits
FLORIDA					
Florida State University Tallahassee, Fla. 32306 (904) 644-1079	64	68	65	74	71	50
University of Miami Coral Gables, Fla. 33146 (305) 284-2673	58	58	60	50	76	n/a
University of Florida Gainesville, Fla. 32611 (352) 375-4683	63	57	50	68	53	67
GEORGIA					
Georgia Institute of Tech. Atlanta, Ga. 30332 (404) 894-5411	67	68	63	90	48	100
University of Georgia Athens, Ga. 30613 (706) 542-9037	60	51	42	68	32	33
HAWAII					
University of Hawaii Honolulu, Hawaii 96822 (808) 956-7301	72	71	68	76	64	100
ILLINOIS					
Northern Illinois University DeKalb, Ill. 60115 (815) 753-0888	51	50	30	81	19	67
Northwestern University Evanston, Ill. 60208 (708) 491-8880	91	93	93	92	92	100
University of Illinois Champaign, Ill. 61820 (217) 333-3631	78	76	79	70	86	33
INDIANA					
Ball State University Muncie, Ind. 47306 (317) 285-1671	55	73	63	85	61	33

Percentage Graduating by 1994

	'90 freshman	'90 freshman athletes	male athletes	female athletes	'90 football recruits	'90 basketball recruits
Indiana University Bloomington, Ind. 47405 (812) 855-1966	70	65	59	83	65	100
Purdue University West Lafayette, Ind. 47907 (317) 494-3189	69	64	55	88	43	50
University of Notre Dame Notre Dame, Ind. 46556 (219) 631-6107	93	93	88	100	87	100
IOWA						
Iowa State University Ames, Iowa 50011 (515) 294-0123	60	62	57	73	64	67
University of Iowa Iowa City, Iowa 52242 (319) 335-9435	63	68	62	77	61	33
KANSAS						
Kansas State University Manhattan, Kan. 66506 (913) 532-6912	48	48	43	57	56	100
University of Kansas Lawrence, Kan. 66045 (913) 864-3143	56	56	51	64	41	67
KENTUCKY						
University of Kentucky Lexington, Ky. 40506 (606) 257-8000	50	48	41	61	43	0
University of Louisville Louisville, Ky. 40292 (502) 588-5732	26	54	45	72	35	0
LOUISIANA						
Louisiana State University Baton Rouge, La. 70803 (504) 388-3600	47	32	27	42	20	0
Louisiana Tech University Ruston, La. 71272 (318) 257-3247	39	35	35	36	30	25

| | Percentage Graduating by 1994 | | | | | |
	'90 freshman	'90 freshman athletes	male athletes	female athletes	'90 football recruits	'90 basketball recruits
Tulane University New Orleans, La. 70118 (504) 865-5501	72	75	71	92	74	100
Univ. of SW Louisiana Lafayette, La. 70504 (318) 482-5393	27	41	38	50	29	50
MARYLAND						
United States Naval Acad. Annapolis, Md. 21402 (410) 293-2429	76	—	—	—	—	—
University of Maryland College Park, Md. 20740 (301) 314-7075	61	69	67	72	72	0
MASSACHUSETTS						
Boston College Chestnut Hill, Mass. 02167 (617) 552-4681	86	90	86	100	84	100
MICHIGAN						
Central Michigan University Mount Pleasant, Mich. 48859 (517) 774-3046	51	63	62	66	73	25
Eastern Michigan University Ypsilanti, Mich. 48197 (313) 487-1050	32	49	50	47	47	25
Michigan State University East Lansing, Mich. 48824 (517) 355-1623	66	74	66	89	44	100
University of Michigan Ann Arbor, Mich. 48109 (313) 764-9416	84	71	58	91	38	33
Western Michigan University Kalamazoo, Mich. 49008 (616) 387-3120	52	47	49	40	36	25
MINNESOTA						
University of Minnesota Minneapolis, Minn. 55455 (612) 625-9579	52	56	50	72	59	25

| | Percentage Graduating by 1994 | | | | | |
	'90 freshman	'90 freshman athletes	male athletes	female athletes	'90 football recruits	'90 basketball recruits
MISSISSIPPI						
Mississippi State University Mississippi State, Miss. 39762 (601) 325-2808	45	51	42	71	62	0
University of Mississippi University, Miss. 38677 (601) 232-7683	47	60	51	83	42	60
Univ. of So. Mississippi Hattiesburg, Miss. 39406 (601) 266-5017	46	67	62	76	60	100
MISSOURI						
University of Missouri Columbia, Mo. 65211 (573) 882-2055	57	58	58	56	60	40
NEBRASKA						
University of Nebraska Lincoln, Neb. 68588 (402) 472-3644	49	61	50	77	63	0
NEVADA						
University of Nevada Las Vegas, Nev. 89154 (702) 895-4729	35	37	25	63	35	0
University of Nevada Reno, Nev. 89557 (702) 784-6900	38	46	40	55	31	100
NEW JERSEY						
Rutgers University New Brunswick, N.J. 08903 (908) 932-8610	75	54	46	67	38	50
NEW MEXICO						
New Mexico State University Las Cruces, N.M. 88003 (505) 646-1211	40	45	26	62	29	n/a
University of New Mexico Albuquerque, N.M. 87131 (505) 277-6375	33	37	36	40	28	67

	Percentage Graduating by 1994					
	'90 freshman	'90 freshman athletes	male athletes	female athletes	'90 football recruits	'90 basketball recruits
NEW YORK						
Syracuse University Syracuse, N.Y. 13244 (315) 443-2385	70	65	63	68	67	50
U.S. Military Academy West Point, N.Y. 10996 (914) 938-3701	86	—	—	—	—	—
NORTH CAROLINA						
Duke University Durham, N.C. 27708 (919) 684-2431	93	91	89	95	86	100
East Carolina University Greenville, N.C. 27858 (919) 328-4501	49	64	57	92	50	67
North Carolina State Univ. Raleigh, N.C. 27695 (919) 515-2109	67	73	64	91	65	100
Univ. of North Carolina Chapel Hill, N.C. 27514 (919) 962-6000	82	63	51	82	48	60
Wake Forest University Winston-Salem, N.C. 27109 (910) 759-5616	85	71	69	80	70	67
OHIO						
Bowling Green State Univ. Bowling Green, Ohio 43403 (419) 372-2401	62	71	71	71	82	33
Kent State University Kent, Ohio 44242 (330) 672-3120	43	61	62	59	53	67
Miami University Oxford, Ohio 45056 (513) 529-3113	82	67	63	76	63	25
Ohio State University Columbus, Ohio 43210 (614) 292-7572	55	49	40	69	29	0

	'90 freshman	'90 freshman athletes	male athletes	female athletes	'90 football recruits	'90 basketball recruits
Percentage Graduating by 1994						
Ohio University Athens, Ohio 45701 (614) 593-0983	68	66	67	63	81	50
University of Akron Akron, Ohio 44325 (216) 972-7080	34	53	35	82	41	100
University of Cincinnati Cincinnati, Ohio 45221 (513) 556-4603	46	48	39	67	37	0
University of Toledo Toledo, Ohio 43606 (419) 530-4987	37	51	47	59	53	50
OKLAHOMA						
Oklahoma State Univ. Stillwater, Okla. 74078 (405) 744-7740	48	41	33	67	44	n/a
University of Oklahoma Norman, Okla. 73019 (405) 325-8241	44	46	35	81	42	0
University of Tulsa Tulsa, Okla. 74104 (918) 631-2357	59	57	60	53	41	33
OREGON						
Oregon State University Corvallis, Ore. 97331 (503) 737-2547	63	61	58	67	63	33
University of Oregon Eugene, Ore. 97403 (541) 346-5464	56	56	49	69	57	33
PENNSYLVANIA						
Pennsylvania State Univ. University Park, Pa. 16802 (814) 865-1086	78	81	72	96	71	50
Temple University Philadelphia, Pa. 19122 (215) 204-7447	49	53	47	65	45	0

| | Percentage Graduating by 1994 | | | | | |
	'90 freshman	'90 freshman athletes	male athletes	female athletes	'90 football recruits	'90 basketball recruits
University of Pittsburgh Pittsburgh, Pa. 15260 (412) 648-8230	62	49	44	63	63	0
SOUTH CAROLINA						
Clemson University Clemson, S.C. 29634 (803) 656-2218	70	41	39	50	45	17
Univ. of South Carolina Columbia, S.C. 29208 (803) 777-8881	63	73	76	62	65	0
TENNESSEE						
University of Memphis Memphis, Tenn. 38152 (901) 678-2335	34	59	50	77	64	n/a
University of Tennessee Knoxville, Tenn. 37996 (615) 974-1224	55	44	38	56	25	0
Vanderbilt University Nashville, Tenn. 37212 (615) 322-4831	82	79	74	89	86	25
TEXAS						
Baylor University Waco, Texas 76798 (817) 755-1234	69	60	53	79	60	33
Rice University Houston, Texas 77251 (713) 527-9851	90	74	67	89	48	100
Southern Methodist Univ. Dallas, Texas 75275 (214) 768-4301	72	72	74	64	65	100
Texas A&M University College Station, Texas 77843 (409) 845-2227	68	53	42	76	26	0
Texas Christian University Fort Worth, Texas 76129 (817) 921-7965	59	39	41	33	44	25

	Percentage Graduating by 1994				
	'90			'90	'90
'90	freshman	male	female	football	basketball
freshman	athletes	athletes	athletes	recruits	recruits
Texas Tech University Lubbock, Texas 79409 (806) 742-3355	42	51	39	72	46	0
University of Houston Houston, Texas 77204 (713) 743-9370	35	33	28	42	259	100
Univ. of Texas at Austin Austin, Texas 78712 (512) 471-5757	63	58	51	70	56	0
Univ. of Texas at El Paso El Paso, Texas 79968 (915) 747-5347	24	32	31	33	36	0
UTAH						
Brigham Young Univ. Provo, Utah 84602 (801) 378-6164	58	59	54	72	48	50
University of Utah Salt Lake City, Utah 84112 (801) 581-5605	38	55	48	67	22	0
Utah State University Logan, Utah 84322 (801) 797-2060	50	41	33	47	33	0
VIRGINIA						
University of Virginia Charlottesville, Va. 22903 (804) 982-5100	91	83	77	94	80	0
Virginia Polytechnic Inst. Blacksburg, Va. 24061 (540) 231-6796	73	62	55	100	50	100
WASHINGTON						
University of Washington Seattle, Wash. 98195 (206) 543-2212	69	57	48	84	59	33
Washington State Univ. Pullman, Wash. 99164 (509) 335-0200	63	58	47	68	41	100

	Percentage Graduating by 1994					
	'90 freshman	'90 freshman athletes	male athletes	female athletes	'90 football recruits	'90 basketball recruits
WEST VIRGINIA						
West Virginia University Morgantown, W.Va. 26506 (304) 293-5621	56	52	45	67	42	67
WISCONSIN						
University of Wisconsin Madison, Wis. 53711 (608) 262-5068	72	56	48	78	63	67
WYOMING						
University of Wyoming Laramie, Wyo. 82071 (307) 766-2292	45	37	34	43	30	100

NCAA, Division I

These schools, while not competing at the highest level in football, still have major sports programs – many of them centered on men's basketball. A large number compete in football at the I-AA level, which includes a year-end national championship playoff. The others – marked with **an asterisk (*)** in the football section of the graduation rate survey – either have no football programs or played Division III football until the 1993-94 school year, when the rules were changed to bar this. These schools do not offer scholarships for football players. Division I teams must offer at least seven varsity sports for men or mixed teams and seven for women (indoor and outdoor track can be counted as two sports). With few exceptions, such as the Ivy League, athletic scholarships are available in most sports. Dashes in the table denote those schools with no athletic aid. Missing information is denoted by n/a on the charts. In some cases this means no freshmen were recruited in a particular sport in 1990-91. In others, the school moved up to Division I too recently to have the required data.

Percentage Graduating by 1994

	'90 freshman	'90 freshman athletes	male athletes	female athletes	'90 football recruits	'90 basketball recruits
ALABAMA						
Alabama State University Montgomery, Ala. 36101 (334) 293-4507	21	50	50	50	46	100
Jacksonville State University Jacksonville, Ala., 36265 (205) 782-5368	29	26	21	100	20	n/a
Samford University Birmingham, Ala. 35229 (205) 870-2131	64	64	59	80	60	0
Troy State University Troy, Ala. 36082 (334) 670-3480	37	56	33	86	33	0
U. of Alabama at Birmingham Birmingham, Ala. 35294 (205) 934-3402	31	37	38	36	*	20
University of South Alabama Mobile, Ala. 36688 (334) 460-7121	30	42	50	35	*	0

| | **Percentage Graduating by 1994** | | | | |
	'90 freshman	'90 freshman athletes	male athletes	female athletes	'90 football recruits	'90 basketball recruits

ARIZONA

Northern Arizona University Flagstaff, Ariz. 86011 (520) 523-5353	39	43	38	50	32	25

ARKANSAS

University of Arkansas Little Rock, Ark. 72204 (501) 569-3167	18	16	12	20	*	0

CALIFORNIA

Calif. Polytechnic State U. San Luis Obispo, Calif. 93407 (805) 756-2923	56	56	52	64	75	50
California State University Fullerton, Calif. 92831 (714) 773-2777	36	24	19	36	0	33
California State University Northridge, Calif. 91330 (818) 885-3208	31	39	30	54	33	67
California State University Sacramento, Calif. 95819 (916) 278-6348	36	56	50	60	n/a	n/a
Long Beach State University Long Beach, Calif. 90840 (310) 985-7976	29	33	25	45	13	33
Loyola Marymount Univ. Los Angeles, Calif. 90045 (310) 338-2765	74	75	57	89	*	50
Pepperdine University Malibu, Calif. 90263 (310) 456-4242	69	79	60	100	*	67
St. Mary's College Moraga, Calif. 94575 (510) 631-4383	68	68	45	80	*	100
Santa Clara University Santa Clara, Calif. 95053 (408) 554-5344	80	61	52	88	50	67

	Percentage Graduating by 1994				
	'90 freshman	'90 freshman athletes	male athletes	female athletes	'90 football recruits	'90 basketball recruits
University of California Irvine, Calif. 92697 (714) 856-6932	72	41	32	60	*	0
University of California Santa Barbara, Calif. 93106 (805) 893-3400	70	73	72	75	*	100
University of San Diego San Diego, Calif. 92110 (619) 260-2930	67	70	64	78	*	100
University of San Francisco San Francisco, Calif. 94117 (415) 422-6891	61	68	67	69	*	50
CONNECTICUT						
Central Connecticut State U. New Britain, Conn. 06050 (860) 832-3035	47	45	29	75	n/a	100
Fairfield University Fairfield, Conn. 06430 (203) 254-4040	83	88	100	67	*	100
University of Connecticut Storrs, Conn. 06269 (860) 486-2725	68	70	61	83	74	0
University of Hartford West Hartford, Conn. 06117 (860) 768-4989	50	68	71	64	*	100
Yale University New Haven, Conn. 06520 (203) 432-1414	93	—	—	—	—	—
DELAWARE						
Delaware State University Dover, Del. 19901 (302) 739-4928	30	52	47	75	40	n/a
University of Delaware Newark, Del. 19716 (302) 831-4006	71	63	56	83	67	0

	Percentage Graduating by 1994				
'90 freshman	'90 freshman athletes	male athletes	female athletes	'90 football recruits	'90 basketball recruits

DISTRICT OF COLUMBIA

American University
Washington, D.C. 20016
(202) 885-30001

| 67 | 74 | 59 | 86 | * | 50 |

George Washington Univ.
Washington, D.C. 20052
(202) 994-6650

| 65 | 79 | 60 | 100 | * | 100 |

Georgetown University
Washington, D.C. 20057
(202) 687-2435

| 90 | 88 | 88 | 88 | * | 67 |

Howard University
Washington, D.C. 20059
(202) 806-2100

| 47 | 51 | 47 | 80 | 55 | n/a |

FLORIDA

Bethune-Cookman College
Daytona Beach, Fla. 32114
(904) 257-2011

| 30 | 44 | 42 | 50 | 44 | 33 |

Florida A&M University
Tallahassee, Fla. 32307
(904) 599-3868

| 42 | 48 | 47 | 50 | 45 | 100 |

Florida Atlantic University
Boca Raton, Fla. 33431
(561) 367-3710

| 47 | 69 | 86 | 56 | * | 80 |

Florida International Univ.
Miami, Fla. 33199
(305) 348-1919

| 55 | 45 | 38 | 56 | * | 0 |

Jacksonville University
Jacksonville, Fla. 32211
(904) 745-7400

| 41 | 44 | 46 | 40 | * | 50 |

Stetson University
DeLand, Fla. 32720
(904) 822-8100

| 64 | 58 | 38 | 72 | * | 25 |

Univ. of Central Florida
Orlando, Fla. 32816
(407) 823-2261

| 51 | 52 | 47 | 69 | 42 | 50 |

Univ. of South Florida
Tampa, Fla. 33620
(813) 974-2125

| 46 | 39 | 35 | 43 | * | 0 |

	Percentage Graduating by 1994					
	'90 freshman	'90 freshman athletes	male athletes	female athletes	'90 football recruits	'90 basketball recruits

GEORGIA

	'90 freshman	'90 freshman athletes	male athletes	female athletes	'90 football recruits	'90 basketball recruits
Georgia Southern Univ. Statesboro, Ga. 30460 (912) 681-5047	40	47	48	43	50	0
Georgia State University Atlanta, Ga. 30303 (404) 651-2772	41	54	62	45	*	100
Mercer University Macon, Ga. 31207 (912) 752-2994	43	37	25	53	*	50

IDAHO

Boise State University Boise, Idaho 83725 (208) 385-1981	25	26	26	26	36	0
Idaho State University Pocatello, Idaho 83209 (208) 236-4064	36	43	33	67	25	33
University of Idaho Moscow, Idaho 83843 (208) 885-0200	47	41	26	70	36	0

ILLINOIS

Bradley University Peoria, Ill. 61625 (309) 677-2670	68	56	47	63	*	0
Chicago State University Chicago, Ill. 60628 (312) 995-3661	16	27	33	20	*	n/a
DePaul University Chicago, Ill. 60604 (312) 325-7502	58	88	83	91	*	100
Eastern Illinois University Charleston, Ill. 61920 (217) 581-3221	69	63	63	64	42	100
Illinois State University Normal, Ill. 61761 (309) 438-3636	54	67	63	73	67	100

		Percentage Graduating by 1994				
	'90 freshman	'90 freshman athletes	male athletes	female athletes	'90 football recruits	'90 basketball recruits
Loyola University Chicago, Ill. 60626 (312) 508-2560	66	83	82	85	*	60
Northeastern Illinois U. Chicago, Ill. 60625 (773) 794-3081	9	33	57	18	*	50
Southern Illinois Univ. Carbondale, Ill. 62901 (618) 453-7250	39	57	55	60	63	33
Univ. of Illinois, Chicago Chicago, Ill. 60607 (312) 996-2695	34	74	68	86	*	50
Western Illinois Univ. Macomb, Ill. 61455 (309) 298-1106	47	59	56	64	69	0
INDIANA						
Butler University Indianapolis, Ind. 46208 (317) 940-9440	62	80	80	81	*	67
University of Evansville Evansville, Ind. 47722 (812) 479-2238	59	67	50	89	*	67
Indiana State University Terre Haute, Ind. 47809 (812) 237-4040	36	49	44	54	58	14
Valparaiso University Valparaiso, Ind. 46383 (219) 464-5230	72	76	73	88	67	80
IOWA						
Drake University Des Moines, Iowa 50311 (515) 271-2889	61	60	44	77	*	29
Univ. of Northern Iowa Cedar Falls, Iowa 50614 (319) 273-2470	59	70	60	85	57	100

| | **Percentage Graduating by 1994** | | | | | |
	'90 freshman	'90 freshman athletes	male athletes	female athletes	'90 football recruits	'90 basketball recruits
KANSAS						
Wichita State University Wichita, Kan. 67260 (316) 689-3250	27	50	52	48	n/a	50
KENTUCKY						
Eastern Kentucky Univ. Richmond, Ky. 40475 (606) 622-1682	25	47	36	67	21	67
Morehead State Univ. Morehead, Ky. 40351 (606) 783-2088	40	54	48	80	46	100
Murray State University Murray, Ky. 42071 (502) 762-6184	46	43	46	38	50	0
Western Kentucky Univ. Bowling Green, Ky. 42101 (502) 745-3542	41	35	30	56	29	0
LOUISIANA						
Centenary College Shreveport, La. 71134 (318) 869-5275	54	54	56	50	*	67
Grambling State Univ. Grambling, La. 71245 (318) 274-2374	33	47	50	40	50	25
McNeese State University Lake Charles, La. 70609 (318) 475-5216	28	34	36	27	32	67
Nicholls State University Thibodaux, La. 70310 (504) 448-4795	19	38	33	45	31	n/a
Northeast Louisiana Univ. Monroe, La. 71209 (318) 342-5361	30	32	29	39	18	0
Northwestern State Univ. Natchitoches, La. 71497 (318) 357-5251	28	34	39	20	23	50

	Percentage Graduating by 1994					
	'90 freshman	'90 freshman athletes	male athletes	female athletes	'90 football recruits	'90 basketball recruits
Southeastern Louisiana U. Hammond, La. 70402 (504) 549-2253	27	46	38	75	*	50
Southern University Baton Rouge, La. 70813 (504) 771-3170	22	41	31	62	0	0
University of New Orleans New Orleans, La. 70148 (504) 286-7020	26	37	25	60	*	0
MAINE						
University of Maine Orono, Maine 04469 (207) 581-1057	54	43	38	54	42	33
MARYLAND						
Coppin State College Baltimore, Md. 21216 (410) 383-5688	23	37	29	60	*	0
Loyola College Baltimore, Md. 21210 (410) 617-5014	78	78	73	81	*	50
Morgan State University Baltimore, Md. 21239 (410) 319-3009	31	37	34	50	19	33
Mount St. Mary's College Emmitsburg, Md. 21727 (301) 447-5000	65	83	83	83	*	67
Towson State University Towson, Md. 21204 (410) 830-2758	58	62	63	61	58	75
U. of Md., Baltimore County Baltimore, Md. 21250 (410) 455-2207	45	59	52	67	*	0
Univ. of Md., Eastern Shore Princess Anne, Md. 21853 (410) 651-6496	30	50	33	80	*	0

		Percentage Graduating by 1994				
	'90 freshman	'90 freshman athletes	male athletes	female athletes	'90 football recruits	'90 basketball recruits

MASSACHUSETTS

Boston University
Boston, Mass. 02215
(617) 353-4630
69 · 77 · 72 · 87 · 78 · 67

College of the Holy Cross
Worcester, Mass. 01610
(508) 793-2582
90 · 80 · 79 · 86 · 80 · 67

Harvard University
Cambridge, Mass. 02138
(617) 495-2204
97 · — · — · — · — · —

Northeastern University
Boston, Mass. 02115
(617) 373-2631
40 · 67 · 70 · 65 · 90 · 100

Univ. of Massachusetts
Amherst, Mass. 01003
(413) 545-4086
60 · 68 · 60 · 82 · 63 · 50

MICHIGAN

Univ. of Detroit Mercy
Detroit, Mich. 48219
(313) 993-1720
37 · 68 · 83 · 50 · * · n/a

MISSISSIPPI

Alcorn State University
Lorman, Miss. 39096
(601) 877-6509
32 · 38 · 37 · 43 · 33 · 0

Jackson State University
Jackson, Miss. 39217
(601) 968-2291
33 · 47 · 36 · 71 · 50 · 14

Mississippi Valley State U.
Itta Bena, Miss. 38941
(601) 254-3551
53 · 52 · 57 · 33 · 64 · 0

MISSOURI

St. Louis University
St. Louis, Mo. 63108
(314) 658-3167
60 · 68 · 50 · 80 · * · 0

Southeast Mo. State Univ.
Cape Girardeau, Mo. 63701
(573) 651-2227
37 · 53 · 45 · 60 · 54 · 100

	Percentage Graduating by 1994					
	'90 freshman	'90 freshman athletes	male athletes	female athletes	'90 football recruits	'90 basketball recruits
Southwest Mo. State U. Springfield, Mo. 65804 (417) 836-5244	39	45	36	62	36	0
University of Missouri Kansas City, Mo. 64110 (816) 235-1048	44	38	17	50	*	33
MONTANA						
Montana State University Bozeman, Mont. 59717 (406) 994-4221	42	50	43	64	50	0
University of Montana Missoula, Mont. 59812 (406) 243-5331	38	52	50	56	50	33
NEBRASKA						
Creighton University Omaha, Neb. 68178 (402) 280-2720	67	59	44	77	*	25
NEW HAMPSHIRE						
Dartmouth College Hanover, N.H. 03755 (603) 646-2465	93	—	—	—	—	—
Univ. of New Hampshire Durham, N.H. 03824 (603) 862-2014	73	75	73	79	78	75
NEW JERSEY						
Fairleigh Dickinson Univ. Teaneck, N.J. 07666 (201) 692-9867	22	47	35	67	*	33
Monmouth University West Long Branch, N.J. 07764 (908) 571-3415	45	47	29	69	*	50
Princeton University Princeton, N.J. 08544 (609) 258-3535	94	—	—	—	—	—
Rider College Lawrenceville, N.J. 08648 (609) 896-5054	55	74	76	72	*	80

		Percentage Graduating by 1994			
	'90 freshman	'90 freshman athletes	male athletes	female athletes	'90 football recruits	'90 basketball recruits
St. Peter's College Jersey City, N.J. 07306 (201) 915-9098	47	51	58	36	*	n/a
Seton Hall University South Orange, N.J. 07079 (201) 761-9497	65	70	61	84	*	33
NEW YORK						
Buffalo State U. of New York Buffalo, N.Y. 14260 (716) 645-3454	60	59	60	57	*	0
Canisius College Buffalo, N.Y. 14208 (716) 888-2970	55	64	50	82	*	100
Colgate University Hamilton, N.Y. 13346 (315) 824-7611	88	82	79	92	71	100
Columbia U./Barnard Coll. New York, N.Y. 10027 (212) 854-2537	84	—	—	—	—	—
Cornell University Ithaca, N.Y. 14853 (607) 255-7595	89	—	—	—	—	—
Fordham University Bronx, N.Y. 10458 (718) 817-4300	74	69	67	100	71	100
Hofstra University Hempstead, N.Y. 11550 (516) 463-6750	61	53	44	63	*	0
Iona College New Rochelle, N.Y. 10801 (914) 633-2311	59	59	61	55	*	33
Long Island U./ **Brooklyn Campus** Brooklyn, N.Y. 11201 (718) 488-1030	27	73	64	100	*	40
Manhattan College Riverdale, N.Y. 10471 (718) 920-0230	71	93	92	93	*	100

	Percentage Graduating by 1994				
	'90 freshman	'90 freshman athletes	male athletes	female athletes	'90 football recruits	'90 basketball recruits
---	---	---	---	---	---	---
Marist College Poughkeepsie, N.Y. 12601 (914) 575-3304	61	54	50	67	*	50
Niagara University Niagara, N.Y. 14109 (716) 286-8601	48	61	64	59	*	60
St. Bonaventure University St. Bonaventure, N.Y. 14778 (716) 375-2282	72	80	81	78	*	75
St. Francis College Brooklyn Heights, N.Y. 11201 (718) 522-2300	39	53	25	78	*	n/a
St. John's University Jamaica, N.Y. 11439 (718) 990-6224	63	75	73	81	*	100
Siena College Loudonville, N.Y. 12211 (518) 783-2551	81	83	67	100	*	67
Wagner College Staten Island, N.Y. 10301 (718) 390-3433	70	68	57	82	*	50
NORTH CAROLINA						
Appalachian State Univ. Boone, N.C. 28608 (704) 262-4010	64	60	57	67	43	100
Campbell University Buies Creek, N.C. 27506 (910) 893-1326	41	50	36	88	*	60
Davidson College Davidson, N.C. 28036 (704) 892-2373	89	79	50	100	n/a	50
North Carolina A&T State U. Greensboro, N.C. 27411 (910) 334-7686	44	31	24	75	32	n/a
Univ. of North Carolina Asheville, N.C. 28804 (704) 251-6459	41	32	29	38	*	17

| | Percentage Graduating by 1994 | | | | | |
	'90 freshman	'90 freshman athletes	male athletes	female athletes	'90 football recruits	'90 basketball recruits
Univ. of North Carolina Charlotte, N.C. 28223 (704) 547-4920	53	51	38	77	*	75
Univ. of North Carolina Greensboro, N.C. 27412 (910) 334-3000	46	43	32	64	*	100
Univ. of North Carolina Wilmington, N.C. 28403 (910) 395-3230	57	69	67	73	*	100
Western Carolina Univ. Cullowhee, N.C. 28723 (704) 227-7338	48	49	46	100	50	17
OHIO						
Cleveland State Univ. Cleveland, Ohio 44115 (216) 687-4808	28	54	43	68	*	29
University of Dayton Dayton, Ohio 45469 (513) 229-2100	75	78	57	100	*	50
Wright State University Dayton, Ohio 45435 (513) 873-2771	32	62	69	52	*	100
Xavier University Cincinnati, Ohio 45207 (513) 745-3413	69	83	80	91	*	100
Youngstown State Univ. Youngstown, Ohio 44555 (330) 742-2385	34	64	65	61	67	25
OKLAHOMA						
Oral Roberts University Tulsa, Okla. 74171 (918) 495-7100	n/a	n/a	n/a	n/a	*	n/a
OREGON						
University of Portland Portland, Ore. 97203 (503) 283-7117	60	57	42	78	*	20

	Percentage Graduating by 1994					
	'90 freshman	'90 freshman athletes	male athletes	female athletes	'90 football recruits	'90 basketball recruits
PENNSYLVANIA						
Bucknell University Lewisburg, Pa. 17837 (717) 524-3301	92	96	95	100	91	100
Drexel University Philadelphia, Pa. 19104 (215) 590-8945	47	75	64	90	*	100
Duquesne University Pittsburgh, Pa. 15282 (412) 396-6565	69	71	62	88	*	33
La Salle University Philadelphia, Pa. 19141 (215) 951-1516	70	79	82	75	*	0
Lafayette College Easton, Pa. 18042 (610) 250-5470	87	86	84	92	76	100
Lehigh University Bethlehem, Pa. 18015 (215) 758-4320	85	90	83	93	88	100
Robert Morris College Coraopolis, Pa. 15108 (412) 262-8302	47	50	55	43	*	33
St. Francis College Loretto, Pa. 15940 (814) 472-3276	53	62	44	81	*	80
St. Joseph's University Philadelphia, Pa. 19131 (610) 660-1707	73	89	93	86	*	100
Univ. of Pennsylvania Philadelphia, Pa. 19104 (215) 898-6121	88	—	—	—	—	—
Villanova University Villanova, Pa. 19085 (610) 519-4111	84	77	74	82	73	50
RHODE ISLAND						
Brown University Providence, R.I. 02912 (401) 863-2348	91	—	—	—	—	—

		Percentage Graduating by 1994			
	'90 freshman athletes	male athletes	female athletes	'90 football recruits	'90 basketball recruits
	'90 freshman				

	'90 freshman	'90 freshman athletes	male athletes	female athletes	'90 football recruits	'90 basketball recruits
Providence College Providence, R.I. 02918 (401) 874-5278	93	86	82	90	*	80
University of Rhode Island Kingston, R.I. 02881 (401) 792-5245	61	58	62	53	88	20
SOUTH CAROLINA						
Charleston Southern U. Charleston, S.C. 29423 (803) 863-7679	33	39	47	32	*	0
The Citadel Charleston, S.C. 29409 (803) 953-5030	77	86	86	n/a	77	100
Coastal Carolina College Conway, S.C. 29528 (803) 349-2820	31	43	29	67	*	0
College of Charleston Charleston, S.C. 29424 (803) 953-8254	56	83	91	50	*	100
Furman University Greenville, S.C. 29613 (864) 294-2150	76	73	64	93	63	0
South Carolina State U. Orangeburg, S.C. 29117 (803) 536-7242	49	53	42	90	45	0
Wofford College Spartansburg, S.C. 29303 (864) 597-4090	84	90	88	100	89	100
Winthrop University Rock Hill, S.C. 29733 (803) 323-2129	57	70	69	72	*	75
TENNESSEE						
Austin Peay State University Clarksville, Tenn. 37044 (615) 648-7903	35	50	52	44	50	0
East Tennessee State U. Johnson City, Tenn. 37614 (423) 439-4343	37	48	39	75	36	0

	Percentage Graduating by 1994					
	'90 freshman	'90 freshman athletes	male athletes	female athletes	'90 football recruits	'90 basketball recruits
Middle Tennessee State U. Murfreesboro, Tenn. 37132 (615) 898-2450	38	31	25	44	30	0
Tennessee State University Nashville, Tenn. 37209 (615)963-5915	32	19	10	57	12	0
Tennessee Tech. U. Cookeville, Tenn. 38505 (615) 372-3242	44	48	39	73	33	25
Univ. of Tenn. at Chattanooga Chattanooga, Tenn. 37403 (423) 755-4495	38	50	55	40	50	100
Univ. of Tenn. at Martin Martin, Tenn. 38238 (901) 587-7660	37	44	40	57	50	n/a
TEXAS						
Lamar University Beaumont, Texas 77710 (409) 880-8323	22	38	36	40	n/a	100
Prairie View A&M University Prairie View, Texas 77446 (409) 857-2127	34	100	0	100	n/a	n/a
Sam Houston University Huntsville, Texas 77341 (409) 294-1726	28	43	36	58	33	33
Southwest Texas State U. San Marcos, Texas 78666 (512) 245-2114	30	43	38	58	39	50
Stephen F. Austin State U. Nacogdoches, Texas 75962 (409) 568-3501	41	39	29	71	30	0
Texas Southern University Houston, Texas 77004 (713) 313-7271	12	24	23	29	37	0
University of North Texas Denton, Texas 76203 (817) 565-3646	35	41	38	47	31	25

	'90 freshman	'90 freshman athletes	Percentage Graduating by 1994 male athletes	female athletes	'90 football recruits	'90 basketball recruits
Univ. of Texas at Arlington Arlington, Texas 76019 (817) 273-5039	27	42	22	31	*	100
Univ. of Texas, Pan American Edinburg, Texas 78539 (210) 381-2221	20	21	14	33	*	0
U. of Texas at San Antonio San Antonio, Texas 78249 (210) 458-4444	24	32	26	39	*	0
UTAH						
Southern Utah University Cedar City, Utah 84720 (801) 586-7828	42	46	50	42	50	n/a
Weber State University Ogden, Utah 84408 (801) 626-6817	40	38	38	38	40	67
VERMONT						
University of Vermont Burlington, Vt. 05405 (802) 656-3075	72	77	75	79	*	67
VIRGINIA						
George Mason University Fairfax, Va. 22030 (703) 993-3210	48	62	57	67	*	33
Hampton University Hampton, Va. 23668 (757) 727-5231	53	60	62	50	75	0
James Madison University Harrisonburg, Va. 22807 (540) 568-6164	82	84	76	96	69	100
Liberty University Lynchburg, Va. 24506 (804) 582-2100	37	49	42	73	37	40
Old Dominion University Norfolk, Va. 23529 (757) 683-3369	40	44	29	67	*	25

	Percentage Graduating by 1994				
	'90 freshman	'90 freshman athletes	male athletes	female athletes	'90 football recruits	'90 basketball recruits
---	---	---	---	---	---	---
Radford University Radford, Va. 24142 (540) 831-5228	58	58	50	69	*	50
University of Richmond Richmond, Va. 23173 (804) 289-8371	83	83	78	94	82	75
Virginia Commonwealth U. Richmond, Va. 23284 (804) 828-8110	43	50	43	60	*	0
Virginia Military Institute Lexington, Va. 24450 (540) 464-7521	67	50	50	n/a	42	67
College of William and Mary Williamsburg, Va. 23187 (757) 221-3330	91	73	73	72	77	25
WASHINGTON						
Eastern Washington U. Cheney, Wash. 99004 (509) 359-2463	44	46	41	56	50	0
Gonzaga University Spokane, Wash. 99258 (509) 328-4220	64	50	42	58	*	33
WEST VIRGINIA						
Marshall University Huntington, W.Va. 25755 (304) 696-5408	41	41	35	57	32	50
WISCONSIN						
Marquette University Milwaukee, Wis. 53201 (414) 288-6303	75	75	70	80	*	75
U. of Wisconsin, Green Bay Green Bay, Wis. 54311 (414) 465-2145	41	53	56	52	*	0
U. of Wisconsin, Milwaukee Milwaukee, Wis. 53201 (414) 229-5669	35	51	28	71	*	0

NCAA, Division II

Just a step behind Division I colleges in the size of athletic programs, these schools can be just as competitive in seeking out athletes. Division II schools must offer at least four varsity sports for men or mixed teams and four for women. There are playoffs in all sports, including football, and scholarships are offered in most sports.

ALABAMA

Alabama A&M University	Normal, Ala. 35762	(205) 851-5362	Div. I in men's soccer
Miles College	Birmingham, Ala. 35208	(205) 923-2771	
Tuskegee University	Tuskegee, Ala. 36088	(334) 727-8849	
University of Alabama	Huntsville, Ala. 35899	(205) 895-6144	
Univ. of North Alabama	Florence, Ala. 35632	(205) 760-4397	
Univ. of West Alabama	Livingston, Ala. 35470	(205) 652-3784	

ALASKA

University of Alaska	Anchorage, Alaska 99508	(907) 786-1225	Div. I in ice hockey
University of Alaska	Fairbanks, Alaska 99775	(907) 474-7205	Div. I in ice hockey

ARIZONA

Grand Canyon University	Phoenix, Ariz. 85017	(602) 589-2816	Div. I in baseball

ARKANSAS

Henderson State Univ.	Arkadelphia, Ark. 71999	(501) 223-5161
U. of Central Arkansas	Conway, Ark. 72035	(501) 450-5737

CALIFORNIA

Calif. Poly. State Univ.	Pomona, Calif. 91768	(909) 869-2811	
California State University	Bakersfield, Calif. 93311	(805) 664-2200	Div. I in wrestling
California State University	Chico, Calif. 95929	(916) 898-6470	
Calif. State Univ., Dominguez Hills	Carson, Calif. 90747	(310) 243-3763	
California State University	Hayward, Calif. 94542	(510) 885-3038	
California State University	Los Angeles, Calif. 90032	(213) 343-3080	
California State University	San Bernardino, Ca. 92407	(909) 880-5011	
Calif. State U., Stanislaus	Turlock, Calif. 95382	(209) 667-3566	
Chapman University	Orange, Calif. 92866	(714) 997-6691	
Humboldt State University	Arcata, Calif. 95521	(707) 826-3666	
Notre Dame, College of	Belmont, Calif. 94002	(415) 508-3685	
San Francisco State U.	San Francisco, Ca. 94132	(415) 338-2218	
Sonoma State University	Rohnert Park, Calif. 94928	(707) 664-2521	
University of California	Davis, Calif. 95616	(916) 754-9276	Div I in wrestling, women's gymnastics
University of California	Riverside, Calif. 92521	(909) 787-5496	

COLORADO

Adams State College	Alamosa, Colo. 81102	(719) 587-7401	
Colorado Christian Univ.	Lakewood, Colo. 80226	(303) 202-0100	
Colorado School of Mines	Golden, Colo. 80401	(303) 273-3368	
Fort Lewis College	Durango, Colo. 81301	(970) 247-7571	
Mesa State College	Grand Junction, Colo. 81501	(970) 248-1963	
Metropolitan State Coll. of Denver	Denver, Colo. 80217	(303) 556-8300	
Regis University	Denver, Colo. 80221	(303) 458-4070	
University of Colorado	Colo. Springs, Colo. 80933	(719) 593-3575	
University of Denver	Denver, Colo. 80208	(303) 871-3399	Div I in ice hockey, women's gymnastics
U. of Northern Colorado	Greeley, Colo. 80639	(970) 351-2534	
U. of Southern Colorado	Pueblo, Colo. 81001	(719) 549-2711	
W. State C.of Colorado	Gunnison, Colo. 81231	(970) 943-2079	

CONNECTICUT

Quinnipiac College	Hamden, Conn. 06518	(203) 281-8621	
Sacred Heart University	Fairfield, Conn. 06432	(203) 365-7649	
So. Connecticut State Univ.	New Haven, Conn. 06515	(203) 392-6001	Div. I in men's gymnastics
University of Bridgeport	Bridgeport, Conn. 06601	(203) 576-4059	
University of New Haven	West Haven, Conn. 06516	(203) 932-7020	

DISTRICT OF COLUMBIA

U. of the District of Columbia	Washington, D.C. 20008	(202) 274-5009

FLORIDA

Barry University	Miami Shores, Fla. 33161	(305) 899-3554
Eckerd College	St. Petersburg, Fla. 33733	(813) 864-8252
Fla. Institute of Tech.	Melbourne, Fla. 32901	(407) 768-8000
Florida Southern College	Lakeland, Fla. 33801	(941) 680-4254
Lynn University	Boca Raton, Fla. 33431	(407) 994-0770
Rollins College	Winter Park, Fla. 32789	(407) 646-2198
St. Leo College	St. Leo, Fla. 33574	352) 588-8221
University of North Florida	Jacksonville, Fla. 32224	(904) 646-2833
University of Tampa	Tampa, Fla. 33606	(813) 253-6240
University of West Florida	Pensacola, Fla. 32514	(904) 474-3004

GEORGIA

Albany State College	Albany, Ga. 31705	(912) 430-4754	
Armstrong State College	Savannah, Ga. 31419	(912) 927-5854	
Augusta College	Augusta, Ga. 30910	(706) 737-1626	Div. I in men's golf
Clark Atlanta University	Atlanta, Ga. 30314	(404) 880-8123	
Columbus College	Columbus, Ga. 31907	(706) 568-2204	
Fort Valley State College	Fort Valley, Ga. 31030	(912) 825-6208	
Georgia College	Milledgeville, Ga. 31061	(912) 453-6341	
Kennesaw State Collge	Marietta, Ga. 30061	(770) 423-6284	
Morehouse College	Atlanta, Ga. 30314	(404) 215-2692	

Morris Brown College	Atlanta, Ga. 30314	(404) 220-3618
Paine College	Augusta, Ga. 30901	(706) 821-8200
Savannah State College	Savannah, Ga. 31404	(912) 353-5181
Valdosta College	Valdosta, Ga. 31698	(912) 333-5890
West Georgia State Univ.	Carrollton, Ga. 30118	(770) 836-6533

HAWAII

Chaminade University	Honolulu, Hawaii 96816	(808) 735-4790
University of Hawaii / Hilo	Hilo, Hawaii 96720	(808) 933-3621
Div. I in baseball		

ILLINOIS

Lewis University	Romeoville, Ill. 60446	(815) 836-5249	
Quincy University	Quincy, Ill. 62301	(217) 228-5290	Div. I in men's soccer
St. Francis, College of	Joliet, Ill. 60435	(815) 740-3464	
Southern Illinois University	Edwardsville, Ill. 62026	(618) 692-2871	Div. I in men's soccer

INDIANA

Indiana Univ./Purdue Univ.	Fort Wayne, Ind. 46805	(219) 481-6643
Indiana Univ./Purdue Univ.	Indianapolis, Ind. 46202	(317) 274-0622
Oakland City College	Oakland City, Ind. 47660	(812) 749-1290
St. Joseph's College	Rensselaer, Ind. 47978	(219) 866-6286
University of Indianapolis	Indianapolis, Ind. 46227	(317) 788-3246
U. of Southern Indiana	Evansville, Ind. 47712	(812) 464-1841

IOWA

| Morningside College | Sioux City, Iowa 51106 | (712) 274-5223 |

KANSAS

Emporia State University	Emporia, Kan. 66801	(316) 341-5354
Fort Hays State University	Hays, Kan. 67601	(913) 628-4050
Pittsburg State University	Pittsburg, Kan. 66762	(316) 235-4653
Washburn Univ. of Topeka	Topeka, Kan. 66621	(913) 231-1010

KENTUCKY

Bellarmine College	Louisville, Ky. 40205	(502) 452-8381
Kentucky State University	Frankfort, Ky. 40601	(502) 227-6014
Kentucky Wesleyan U.	Owensboro, Ky. 43202	(502) 926-3111
Northern Kentucky U.	Highland Heights, Ky 41099	(606) 572-5631

MARYLAND

| Bowie State University | Bowie, Md. 20715 | (301) 464-6514 |

MASSACHUSETTS

American Int'l College	Springfield, Mass. 01109	(413) 747-6540
Assumption College	Worcester, Mass. 01615	(508) 767-7279
Bentley College	Waltham, Mass. 02154	(617) 891-2330

Merrimack College	No. Andover, Mass. 01845	(508) 837-5341	Div. I in ice hockey
Springfield College	Springfield, Mass. 01109	(413) 748-3333	Div. I in field hockey
Stonehill College	North Easton, Mass. 02357	(508)565-1023	
Univ. of Mass. at Lowell	Lowell, Mass. 01854	(508) 934-2346	Div. I in ice hockey

MICHIGAN

Ferris State University	Big Rapids, Mich. 49307	(616) 592-2860	Div. I in ice hockey
Grand Valley State Univ.	Allendale, Mich. 49401	(616) 895-3259	
Hillsdale College	Hillsdale, Mich. 49242	(517) 437-7364	
Lake Superior State Univ.	Sault Ste. Marie, Mich. 49783	(906) 635-2627	Div. I in ice hockey
Michigan Tech. Univ.	Houghton, Mich. 49931	(906) 487-3070	Div. I in ice hockey
Northern Michigan Univ.	Marquette, Mich. 49855	(906) 227-1211	Div. I in ice hockey
Northwood Institute	Midland, Mich. 48640	(517) 837-4389	
Oakland University	Rochester, Mich. 48309	(810) 370-3196	
Sagniaw Valley State U.	Univ. Center, Mich. 48710	(517) 791-7300	
Wayne State University	Detroit, Mich. 48202	(313) 577-4280	

MINNESOTA

Bemidji State University	Bemidji, Minn. 56601	(218) 755-2767	
Mankato State University	Mankato, Minn. 56002	(507) 389-1795	
Moorhead State Univ.	Moorhead, Minn. 56563	(218) 236-2306	
St. Cloud State University	St. Cloud, Minn. 56301	(320) 255-3102	Div. I in ice hockey
Southwest State Univ.	Marshall, Minn. 56258	(507) 537-7253	
U. of Minnesota/Duluth	Duluth, Minn. 55812	(218) 726-8718	Div. I in ice hockey
U. of Minnesota/Morris	Morris, Minn. 56267	(320) 589-6421	
Winona State University	Winona, Minn. 55987	(507) 457-5020	

MISSISSIPPI

Delta State University	Cleveland, Miss. 38733	(601) 846-4300
Mississippi College	Clinton, Miss. 39058	(601) 925-3342
Mississippi U.for Women	Columbus, Miss. 39701	(601) 329-7225

MISSOURI

Central Missouri State U.	Warrensburg, Mo. 64093	(816) 543-4521
Drury College	Springfield, Mo. 65802	(417) 873-7294
Lincoln University	Jefferson City, Mo. 65102	(573) 681-5342
Missouri So. State College	Joplin, Mo. 64801	(417) 625-9317
Missouri W.State College	St. Joseph, Mo. 64507	(816) 271-4482
NW Missouri State Univ.	Maryville, Mo. 64468	(816) 562-1306
Southwest Baptist Univ.	Bolivar, Mo. 65613	(573) 326-1749
Truman State University	Kirksville, Mo. 63501	(816) 785-4236
University of Missouri	Rolla, Mo. 65401	(314) 341-4177
University of Missouri	St. Louis, Mo. 63121	(314) 516-5657

MONTANA

Montana State U./Billings	Billings, Mont. 59101	(406) 657-2282

NEBRASKA

Chadron State College	Chadron, Neb. 69337	(308) 432-6345
University of Nebraska	Kearney, Neb. 68849	(308) 865-8514
University of Nebraska	Omaha, Neb. 68182	(402) 554-2533
Wayne State College	Wayne, Neb. 68787	(402) 375-7520

NEW HAMPSHIRE

Franklin Pierce College	Rindge, N.H. 03461	(603) 899-4080
Keene State College	Keene, N.H. 03435	(603) 358-2813
New Hampshire College	Hookset, N.H. 03106	(603) 645-9604
St. Anselm College	Manchester, N.H. 03102	(603) 641-7800

NEW MEXICO

East. New Mexico Univ.	Portales, N.M. 88130	(505) 562-2414
New Mexico Highlands U.	Las Vegas, N.M. 87701	(505) 454-3368
W. New Mexico Univ.	Silver City, N.M. 88061	(505) 538-6234

NEW YORK

Adelphi University	Garden City, N.Y. 11530	(516) 877-4321	Div. I in men's soccer
Concordia College	Bronxville, N.Y. 10708	(914) 337-9300	
Dowling College	Oakdale, N.Y. 11769	(516) 244-3019	
LeMoyne College	Syracuse, N.Y. 13214	(315) 445-4412	Div. I in baseball
Long Island Univ./			
C.W. Post Campus	Brookville, N.Y. 11548	(516) 299-2289	Div. I in baseball
Mercy College	Dobbs Ferry, N.Y. 10522	(914) 674-7504	
Molloy College	Rockville Centre, N.Y. 11571	(516)256-2207	
New York Insti. of Tech.	Old Westbury, N.Y. 11568	(516) 686-7626	Div. I in baseball
Pace University	New York, , N.Y. 10038	(914) 773-3411	Div. I in baseball
Queens College	Flushing, N.Y. 11367	(718) 520-7215	
St. Rose, College of	Albany, N.Y. 12203	(518) 454-5282	
Southampton Campus			
of Long Island U.	Southampton, N.Y. 11968	(516) 287-8386	

NORTH CAROLINA

Barton College	Wilson, N.C. 27893	(919) 399-6517
Belmont Abbey College	Belmont, N.C. 28012	(704) 825-6700
Catawba College	Salisbury, N.C. 28144	(704) 637-4474
Elizabeth City State Univ.	Elizabeth City, N.C. 27909	(919) 335-3396
Elon College	Elon College, N.C. 27244	(910) 584-2420
Fayetteville State Univ.	Fayetteville, N.C. 28301	(910) 486-1314
Gardner-Webb College	Boiling Springs, N.C. 28017	(704) 434-4342
High Point University	High Point, N.C. 27262	(919) 841-9275
Johnson C. Smith Univ.	Charlotte, N.C. 28216	(704) 378-1072
Lees-McRae College	Banner Elk, N.C. 28604	(704) 898-8725
Lenoir-Rhyne College	Hickory, N.C. 28603	(704) 328-7115
Livingstone College	Salisbury, N.C. 28144	(704) 638-5575
Mars Hill College	Mars Hill, N.C. 28754	(704) 689-1219
Mount Olive College	Mount Olive, N.C. 28365	(919) 658-5056
N. Carolina Central Univ.	Durham, N.C. 27707	(919) 560-5427

Pembroke State University	Pembroke, N.C. 28372	(910) 521-6334	
Pfeiffer College	Misenheimer, N.C. 28109	(704) 463-1360	
Queens College	Charlotte, N.C. 28274	(704) 337-2510	
St. Andrew's Presbyterian College	Laurinburg, N.C. 28352	(910) 277-5275	
St. Augustine's College	Raleigh, N.C. 27610	(919) 516-4171	
Shaw University	Raleigh, N.C. 27611	(919) 546-8281	
Wingate College	Wingate, N.C. 28174	(704) 233-8193	
Winston-Salem State U.	Winston-Salem, N.C. 27110	(910) 750-2141	

NORTH DAKOTA

North Dakota State Univ.	Fargo, N.D. 58105	(701) 237-8985	
University of North Dakota	Grand Forks, N.D. 58202	(701) 777-2234	Div. I in ice hockey ‘

OHIO

Ashland University	Ashland, Ohio 44805	(419) 289-5959

OKLAHOMA

Cameron University	Lawton, Okla. 73505	(405) 581-2300
U. of Central Oklahoma	Edmond, Okla. 73034	(405) 341-2980

OREGON

Portland State University	Portland, Ore. 97207	(503) 725-4000	Div. I in baseball

PENNSYLVANIA

Bloomsburg Univ.of Pa. (717) 389-4363	Bloomsburg, Pa. 17815 Div. I in wrestling		
California University of Pa.	California, Pa. 15419	(412) 938-4351	Div. I in wrestling
Cheyney University of Pa.	Cheyney, Pa. 19319	(610) 399-2287	
Clarion University of Pa. Div. I in wrestling	Clarion, Pa. 16214	(814) 226-1997	
E. Stroudsburg U. of Pa. (717) 424-3642	E.Stroudsburg, Pa. 18301 Div. I in wrestling		
Edinboro University of Pa. Div. I in wrestling	Edinboro, Pa. 16444	(814) 732-2776	
Gannon University	Erie, Pa. 16541	(814) 871-5835	
Indiana University of Pa.	Indiana, Pa. 15705	(412) 357-2132	
Kutztown Univ. of Pa.	Kutztown, Pa. 19530	(610) 683-4095	
Lock Haven Univ. of Pa.	Lock Haven, Pa. 17745	(717) 893-2102	Div. I in wrestling
Mansfield Univ. of Pa.	Mansfield, Pa. 16933	(717) 662-4636	
Mercyhurst College	Erie, Pa. 16546	(814) 824-2226	
Millersville Univ. of Pa.	Millersville, Pa. 17551	(717) 872-3361	Div. I in wrestling
Phil. Coll. of Textiles and Science	Philadelphia, Pa. 19144	(215) 951-2720	Div. I in men's soccer
Shippensburg U. of Pa.	Shippensburg, Pa. 17257	(717) 532-1711	
Slippery Rock U. of Pa.	Slippery Rock, Pa. 16057	(412) 738-2767	Div. I in wrestling
U. of Pittsburgh/Johnstown	Johnstown, Pa. 15904	(814) 269-2001	
West Chester U. of Pa.	West Chester, Pa. 19383	(610) 436-3555	Div. I in field hockey

RHODE ISLAND

Bryant College	Smithfield, R.I. 02917	(401) 232-6070

SOUTH CAROLINA

Coker College	Hartsville, S.C. 29550	(803) 383-8071
Erskine College	Due West, S.C. 29639	(864) 379-8859
Francis Marion University	Florence, S.C. 29501	(803) 661-1240
Lander University	Greenwood, S.C. 29649	(864) 388-8314
Limestone College	Gaffney, S.C. 29340	(864) 488-4561
Newberry College	Newberry, S.C. 29108	(803) 321-5155
Presbyterian College	Clinton, S.C. 29325	(803) 833-8242
Univ. of South Carolina/Aiken	Aiken, S.C. 29801	(803) 648-6851
Univ. of South Carolina/ Spartanburg	Spartanburg, S.C. 29303	(864) 503-5141

SOUTH DAKOTA

Augustana College	Sioux Falls, S.D. 57197	(605) 336-4315
Northern State University	Aberdeen, S.D. 57401	(605) 626-2488
South Dakota State Univ.	Brookings, S.D. 57007	(605) 688-5625
University of South Dakota	Vermillion, S.D. 57069	(605) 677-5951

TENNESSEE

Carson-Newman College	Jefferson City, Tenn. 37760	(423) 471-3469
Lane College	Jackson, Tenn. 38301	(901) 426-7568
LeMoyne-Owen College	Memphis, Tenn. 38126	(901) 942-7327
Lincoln Memorial Univ.	Harrogate, Tenn. 37752	(423) 869-6399

TEXAS

Abilene Christian Univ.	Abilene, Texas 79699	(915) 674-2323
Angelo State University	San Angelo, Texas 76909	(915) 942-2091
Houston Baptist Univ.	Houston, Texas 77074	(713) 995-3314
Tarleton State University	Stephenville, Texas 76402	(817) 968-9183
Texas A & M University	Commerce, Texas 75429	(903) 886-5100
Texas A&M University	Kingsville, Texas 78363	(512) 595-2499
Texas Woman's Univ.	Denton, Texas 76201	(817) 898-2378
West Texas A&M Univ.	Canyon, Texas 79016	(806) 656-2069

VERMONT

St. Michael's College	Colchester, Vt. 05439	(802) 654-2502

VIRGINIA

Longwood College	Farmville, Va. 23909	(804) 395-2058
Norfolk State University	Norfolk, Va. 23504	(804) 683-8152
St. Paul's College	Lawrenceville, Va. 23868	(804) 848-2001
Virginia State University	Petersburg, Va. 23806	(804) 524-5030
Virginia Union University	Richmond, Va. 23220	(804)321-1874

WASHINGTON

Seattle Pacific University	Seattle, Wash. 98119	(206) 281-2085

WEST VIRGINIA

Alderson-Broadus College	Philippi, W. Va. 26416	(304) 457-6284
Bluefield State College	Bluefield, W. Va. 25701	(304) 327-4191
Concord College	Athens, W. Va. 24712	(304) 384-5347
Davis and Elkins College	Elkins, W. Va. 26241	(304) 637-1252
Div. I in field hockey		
Fairmont State College	Fairmont, W. Va. 26554	(304) 367-4220
Glenville State College	Glenville, W. Va. 26351	(304) 462-4407
Salem-Teikyo University	Salem, W. Va. 26426	(304) 782-5271
Shepherd College	Shepherdstown,	
	W. Va. 25443	(304) 876-5263
University of Charleston	Charleston, W. Va. 25304	(304) 357-4820
West Liberty State Coll.	West Liberty, W. Va. 26074	(304) 336-8200
W. Virginia Inst. of Tech.	Montgomery, W. Va. 25136	(304) 442-3121
W. Virginia Wesleyan Coll.	Buckhannon, W. Va. 26201	(304) 473-8099
Wheeling Jesuit College	Wheeling, W. Va. 26003	(304) 243-2365

WISCONSIN

University of Wisconsin	Parkside, Wis. 53141	(414) 595-2308

NCAA, Division III

These smaller, often private schools, have no athletic scholarships. Financial aid is offered on the basis of need only, and student-athletes cannot be treated more favorably than other students. Still, many have very competitive sports programs. Division III schools must offer at least four varsity sports for men or mixed teams and four for women. There are playoffs in all sports.

ALABAMA

Stillman College	Tuscaloosa, Ala. 35403	(205)366-8838

ARKANSAS

Hendrix College	Conway, Ark. 72032	(501) 450-1315

CALIFORNIA

California Institute of Tech.	Pasadena, Calif. 91125	(818) 356-6148
California Lutheran Univ.	Thousand Oaks, Calif. 91360	(805) 493-3402
Claremont McKenna-H.Mudd-Scripps	Claremont, Calif. 91711	(909) 607-2220
Menlo College	Atherton, Calif. 94027	(415) 688-3723
Mills College	Oakland, Calif. 94613	510) 430-2172
Occidental College	Los Angeles, Calif. 90041	(213) 259-2708
Pomona-Pitzer Colleges	Claremont, Calif. 91711	(909) 621-8016
U. of Calif., San Diego	La Jolla, Calif. 92093	(619) 534-4211
University of California	Santa Cruz, Calif. 95064	(408) 459-2531
University of La Verne	La Verne, Calif. 91750	(909) 593-3511
University of Redlands	Redlands, Calif. 92373	909) 335-4004
Whittier College	Whittier, Calif. 90608	(310) 907-4268

COLORADO

Colorado College	Colorado Springs, Colo. 80903	(719) 389-6475	Div. I in ice hockey, women's soccer

CONNECTICUT

Albertus Magnus College	New Haven, Conn. 06511	(203) 773-8575
Connecticut College	New London, Conn. 06320	(860) 439-2570
E. Connecticut State Univ.	Willimantic, Conn. 06226	(203) 465-5169
St. Joseph's College	West Hartford, Conn. 06117	(203) 232-3777
Trinity College	Hartford, Conn. 06106	(860) 297-2055
U.S. Coast Guard Acad.	New London, Conn. 06320	860) 444-8600
Wesleyan University	Middletown, Conn. 06459	(860) 685-2896
W. Connecticut State U.	Danbury, Conn. 06810	(203) 797-4239

DELAWARE

Wesley College	Dover, Del. 19901	(302) 736-2557

DISTRICT OF COLUMBIA

Catholic University	Washington, D.C. 20064	(202) 319-6047
Gallaudet University	Washington, D.C. 20002	(202) 651-5603

GEORGIA

Agnes Scott College	Decatur, Ga. 30030	(404) 638-6359
Emory University	Atlanta, Ga. 30322	(404) 727-6532
Oglethorpe University	Atlanta, Ga. 30319	(404) 364-8414
Savannah Coll. of Art and Design	Savannah, Ga. 31402	(912)757-255
Wesleyan Coll. (Georgia)	Macon, Ga. 31297	(912) 477-1110

ILLINOIS

Augustana College	Rock Island, Ill. 61201	(309) 794-7523
Aurora University	Aurora, Ill. 60506	(708) 844-5406
Blackburn College	Carlinville, Ill. 62626	(217) 854-5520
Concordia University	River Forest, Ill. 60305	(708) 209-3028
Elmhurst College	Elmhurst, Ill. 60126	(630) 617-3142
Eureka College	Eureka, Ill. 61530	(309) 467-6373
Illinois Benedictine Univ.	Lisle, Ill. 60532	(630) 829-6150
Illinois College	Jacksonville, Ill. 62650	(217) 245-3393
Illinois Wesleyan Univ.	Bloomington, Ill. 61702	(309) 556-3345
Knox College	Galesburg, Ill. 61401	(309)341-7280
Lake Forest College	Lake Forest, Ill. 60045	(847) 735-5290
MacMurray College	Jacksonville, Ill. 62650	(217) 479-7142
Millikin University	Decatur, Ill. 62522	(217) 424-6344
Monmouth College	Monmouth, Ill. 61462	(309) 457-2176
North Central College	Naperville, Ill. 60566	(630) 637-5500
North Park College	Chicago, Ill. 60625	(312) 244-5676
Parks Coll. of St. Louis U.	Cahokia, Ill. 62206	(618) 337-7500
Principia College	Elsah, Ill. 62028	(618) 374-5025
Rockford College	Rockford, Ill. 61108	(815) 226-4085
University of Chicago	Chicago, Ill. 60637	(773) 702-7684
Wheaton College	Wheaton, Ill. 60187	(630) 752-5125

INDIANA

Anderson University	Anderson, Ind. 46012	(317) 641-4483
DePauw University	Greencastle, Ind. 46135	(317) 658-4934
Earlham College	Richmond, Ind. 47374	(317) 983-1489
Franklin College	Franklin, Ind. 46131	(317) 738-8121
Hanover College	Hanover, Ind. 47243	(812) 866-7374
Manchester College	N. Manchester, Ind. 46962	(219) 982-5214
Rose-Hulman Inst. of Tech.	Terre Haute, Ind. 47803	(812) 877-8270
Saint Mary's College	Notre Dame, Ind. 46556	(219) 284-5548
Wabash College	Crawfordsville, Ind. 47933	(317) 364-6233

IOWA

Buena Vista College	Storm Lake, Iowa 50588	(712) 749-2253
Central College	Pella, Iowa 50219	(515) 628-5310
Coe College	Cedar Rapids, Iowa 52402	(319) 399-8622
Cornell College	Mount Vernon, Iowa 52314	(319) 895-4267
Grinnell College	Grinnell, Iowa 50112	(515) 269-3800
Loras College	Dubuque, Iowa 52004	(319) 588-7112
Luther College	Decorah, Iowa 52101	(319) 387-1575
Simpson College	Indianola, Iowa 50125	(515) 961-1620
University of Dubuque	Dubuque, Iowa 52001	(319) 589-3559
Upper Iowa University	Fayette, Iowa 52142	(319) 425-5227
Wartburg College	Waverly, Iowa 50677	(319) 352-8470
William Penn College	Oskaloosa, Iowa 52577	(515) 673-1023

KENTUCKY

Centre College	Danville, Ky. 40422	(606) 238-5485
Thomas More College	Crestview Hills, Ky. 41017	(606) 344-3536

MAINE

Bates College	Lewiston, Maine 04240	(207) 786-6341
Bowdoin College	Brunswick, Maine 04011	(207) 725-3666
Colby College	Waterville, Maine 04901	(207) 872-3364
Maine Maritime Academy	Castine, Maine 04421	(207) 326-2451
St. Joseph's College	Standish, Maine 04062	(207) 892-6766
Univ. of Southern Maine	Gorham, Maine 04038	(207) 7803988

MARYLAND

Frostburg State University	Frostburg, Md. 21532	(301) 689-4471	
Goucher College	Towson, Md. 21204	(410) 337-6385	
Hood College	Frederick, Md. 21701	(301) 696-3497	
Johns Hopkins University	Baltimore, Md. 21218	(410) 516-7490	Div. I in men's lacrosse
Notre Dame, College of	Baltimore, Md. 21210	(410) 532-3588	
St. Mary's College of MD	St. Mary's City, Md. 20686	(301) 862-0320	
Salisbury State University	Salisbury, Md. 21801	(410) 548-3503	
;Villa Julie College	Stevenson , Md. 21153	(410) 602-7250	
Washington College	Chestertown, Md. 21620	(410) 778-7231	
Western Maryland Coll.	Westminster, Md. 21157	(410) 857-2571	

MASSACHUSETTS

Amherst College	Amherst, Mass. 01002	(413) 542-2274
Anna Maria College	Paxton, Mass. 01612	(508) 849-3447
Babson College	Wellesley, Mass. 02157	(617) 239-4594
Brandeis University	Waltham, Mass. 02254	(617) 736-3630
Bridgewater State Coll.	Bridgewater, Mass. 02325	(508) 697-1352
Clark University	Worcester, Mass. 01610	(508) 793-7160
Curry College	Milton, Mass. 02186	(617) 333 2109
Eastern Nazarene Coll.	Quincy, Mass. 02170	(617) 745-3637
Elms College	Chicopee, Mass. 01013	(413) 594-9474
Emerson College	Boston, Mass. 02116	(617) 578-8690

Emmanuel College	Boston, Mass. 02115	(617) 735-9985
Endicott College	Beverly, Mass. 01915	(508) 232-2304
Fitchburg State College	Fitchburg, Mass. 01420	(508)665-3314
Framingham State Coll.	Framingham, Mass. 01701	(508) 626-4614
Gordon College	Wenham, Mass. 01984	(508) 927-2300
Mass. Institute of Tech.	Cambridge, Mass. 02139	(617) 253-4497
Mass. Maritime Academy	Buzzards Bay, Mass. 02532	(508) 830-5055
Mount Holyoke College	South Hadley, Mass. 01075	(413) 538-2310
Nichols College	Dudley, Mass. 01571	(508) 943-1560
North Adams State College	North Adams, Mass. 01247	(413) 662-5411
Pine Manor College	Chestnut Hill, Mass. 02167	(617) 731-7056
Regis College	Weston, Mass. 02193	(617)768-7147
Salem State College	Salem, Mass. 01970	(508) 741-6570
Simmons College	Boston, Mass. 02115	(617) 521-1038
Smith College	Northampton, Mass. 01063	(413) 585-2701
Suffolk University	Boston, Mass. 02114	(617) 573-8379
Tufts University	Medford, Mass. 02155	(617) 627-3232
Univ. of Massachusetts	Boston, Mass. 02125	(617) 287-7810
Univ. of Massachusetts	N. Dartmouth, Mass. 02747	(508) 999-8722
Wellesley College	Wellesley, Mass. 02181	(617) 283-2001
Wentworth Inst. of Tech.	Boston, Mass. 02115	(617)989-4146
W. New England College	Springfield, Mass. 01119	(413) 782-3111
Westfield State College	Westfield, Mass. 01086	(413) 572-5405
Wheaton College	Norton, Mass. 02766	(508) 285-8216
Williams College	Williamstown, Mass. 01267	(413) 597-2366
Worcester Polytech. Inst.	Worcester, Mass. 01609	(508) 831-5243
Worcester State College	Worcester, Mass. 01602	(508) 793-8034

MICHIGAN

Adrian College	Adrian, Mich. 49221	(517) 265-5161
Albion College	Albion, Mich. 49224	(517) 629-0459
Alma College	Alma, Mich. 48801	(517) 463-7988
Calvin College	Grand Rapids, Mich. 49546	(616) 957-6020
Hope College	Holland, Mich. 49422	(616) 395-7698
Kalamazoo College	Kalamazoo, Mich. 49006	(616) 337-7091
Olivet College	Olivet, Mich. 49076	(616) 749-7672

MINNESOTA

Augsburg College	Minneapolis, Minn. 55454	(612) 330-1016
Bethel College	St. Paul, Minn. 55112	(612) 638-6396
Carleton College	Northfield, Minn. 55057	(507) 663-4056
Concordia College	Moorhead, Minn. 56562	(218) 299-4435
Gustavus Adolphus Coll.	St. Peter, Minn. 56082	(507) 933-7622
Hamline University	St. Paul, Minn. 55104	(612) 641-2326
Macalester College	St. Paul, Minn. 55105	(612) 696-6164
Martin Luther College	New Ulm, Minn. 56073	(507) 354-8221
St. Benedict, College of	St. Joseph, Minn. 56374	(320) 363-5301
St. Catherine, College of	St. Paul, Minn. 55105	(612) 690-8771
St. John's University	Collegeville, Minn. 56321	(612) 363-2500
St. Mary's College	Winona, Minn. 55987	(507) 457-1578
St. Olaf College	Northfield, Minn. 55057	(507) 646-3250

| St. Scholastica, College of | Duluth, Minn. 55811 | (218) 723-6199 |
| University of St. Thomas | St. Paul, Minn. 55105 | (612) 962-5901 |

MISSISSIPPI

| Millsaps College | Jackson, Miss. 39210 | (601) 974-1190 |
| Rust College | Holly Springs, Miss. 38635 | (601) 252-4661 |

MISSOURI

Fontbonne College	St. Louis, Mo. 63105	(314) 889-1444
Maryville College	St. Louis, Mo. 63141	(314) 576-9484
Washington University	St. Louis, Mo. 63130	(314) 935-5288
Webster University	Webster Groves, Mo. 63119	(314) 968-6984
Westminster College	Fulton, Mo. 65251	(573) 642-1200

NEBRASKA

| Nebraska Wesleyan Univ. | Lincoln, Neb. 68504 | (402) 465-2360 |

NEW HAMPSHIRE

Colby-Sawyer College	New London, N.H. 03257	(603) 526-3610
Daniel Webster College	Nashua, N.H. 03063	(603) 577-6495
New England College	Henniker, N.H. 03242	(603) 428-2238
Plymouth State College	Plymouth, N.H. 03264	(603) 535-2751

NEW JERSEY

The College of New Jersey	Trenton, N.J. 08650	(609) 771-2230	
Drew University	Madison, N.J. 07940	(201) 408-3648	
Fairleigh Dickinson Univ.	Madison, N.J. 07940	(201) 443-8960	
Jersey City State College	Jersey City, N.J. 07305	(201) 200-3317	
Kean College	Union, N.J. 07083	(908) 527-2436	
Montclair State College	Upper Montclair, N.J. 07043	(201) 655-5234	
N.J. Institute of Tech.	Newark, N.J. 07102	(201) 596-5727	
Ramapo College	Mahwah, N.J. 07430	(201) 529-7683	
Richard Stockton			
College of New Jersey	Pomona, N.J. 08240	(609) 652-4217	
Rowan C. of New Jersey	Glassboro, N.J. 08028	(609) 256-4686	
Rutgers University	Camden, N.J. 08102	(609) 225-6193	
Rutgers University	Newark, N.J. 07102	(201) 648-5474	Div. I in men's volleyball
St. Elizabeth, College of	Morristown, N.J. 07960	(201)605-7207	
Stevens Institute of Tech.	Hoboken, N.J. 07030	(201) 216-5692	
Upsala College	East Orange, N.J. 07019	(201) 266-7277	
William Paterson College	Wayne, N.J. 07470	(201) 595-2356	

NEW YORK

Albany, State Univ.		
of New York at	Albany, N.Y. 12222	(518) 442-3076
Alfred University	Alfred, N.Y. 14802	(607) 871-2193
Bard College	Annandale-on-Hudson, N.Y. 12504	(914) 758-7528
Bernard M. Baruch Coll.	New York, N.Y. 10010	(212) 387-1271

Binghamton, State Univ. of N.Y. at	Binghamton, N.Y. 13902	(607) 777-4255	
Brockport State U. College	Brockport, N.Y. 14420	(716) 395-2579	
Buffalo State College	Buffalo, N.Y. 14222	(716) 878-6533	
Clarkson University	Potsdam, N.Y. 13699	(315) 268-6616	Div. I in ice hockey
Cortland State U. College	Cortland, N.Y. 13045	(607) 753-4963	
Elmira College	Elmira, N.Y. 14901	(607) 735-1730	
Fredonia State U. College	Fredonia, N.Y. 14063	(716) 673-3101	
Geneseo State U.College	Geneseo, N.Y. 14454	(716) 245-5345	
Hamilton College	Clinton, N.Y. 13323	(315) 859-4115	
Hartwick College	Oneonta, N.Y. 13820	(607) 431-4702	Div. I in men's soccer
Hobart and William Smith Colleges	Geneva, N.Y. 14456	(315) 781-3565	Div. I in men's lacrosse
Hunter College	New York, N.Y. 10021	(212) 772-4783	
Ithaca College	Ithaca, N.Y. 14850	(607) 274-3209	
John Jay Coll. of Criminal Justice	New York, N.Y. 10019	(212) 237-8371	
Keuka College	Keuka Park, N.Y. 14478	(315) 536-5216	
Lehman College	Bronx, N.Y. 10468	(718) 960-1117	
Manhattanville College	Purchase, N.Y. 10577	(914) 323-5281	
Medgar Evers College	Brooklyn, N.Y. 11225	(718) 270-6402	
Mount St. Mary's College	Newburgh, N.Y. 12550	(914) 569-3592	
Mount St. Vincent, Coll. of	Riverdale, N.Y. 10471	(718) 405-3410	
Nazareth College	Rochester, N.Y. 14618	(716) 389-2196	
New Paltz State Univ. College	New Paltz, N.Y. 12561	(914) 257-3923	
New Rochelle, College of	New Rochelle, N.Y. 10805	(914) 654-5315	
New York, City College of	New York, N.Y. 10031	(212) 650-8228	
New York Maritime Coll.	Bronx, N.Y. 10465	(718) 409-7331	
New York University	New York, N.Y. 10012	(212) 998-2040	
Old Westbury State Univ. College	Old Westbury, N.Y. 11568	(516) 876-3241	
Oneonta State U. College	Oneonta, N.Y. 13820	(607) 436-3594	Div. I in men's soccer
Oswego State U. College	Oswego, N.Y. 13126	(315) 341-2378	
Plattsburgh State U. Coll.	Plattsburgh, N.Y. 12901	(518) 564-3140	
Polytechnic University	Brooklyn, N.Y. 11201	(718) 260-3860	
Potsdam State U. College	Potsdam, N.Y. 13676	(315) 267-2305	
Rensselaer Polytech. Inst.	Troy, N.Y. 12180	(518) 276-6685	Div. I in ice hockey
Rochester Inst. of Tech.	Rochester, N.Y. 14623	(716) 475-2615	
Russell Sage College	Troy, N.Y. 12180	(518) 270-2283	
St. John Fisher College	Rochester, N.Y. 14618	(716) 385-8310	
St. Lawrence University	Canton, N.Y. 13617	(315) 379-5877	Div. I in ice hockey
Skidmore College	Saratoga Springs, N.Y. 12866	(518) 584-5000	
Staten Island, College of	Staten Island, N.Y. 10314	(718) 982-3150	
Stony Brook, State Univ. of N.Y.	Stony Brook, N.Y. 11794	(516) 632-7194	Div. I in men's lacrosse, women's soccer
U.S. Merchant Marine Academy	King's Point, N.Y. 11024	(516) 773-5454	

Union College	Schenectady, N.Y. 12308	(518) 388-6284 Div. I in ice hockey
University of Rochester	Rochester, N.Y. 14627	(716) 275-4301
Utica College	Utica, N.Y. 13502	(315) 792-3051
Utica/Rome, SUNY		
Inst. of Tech	Utica, N.Y. 13504	(315) 792-7520
Vassar College	Poughkeepsie, N.Y. 12601	(914) 437-7452
Wells College	Aurora, N.Y. 13026	(315) 364-3410
Yeshiva University	New York, N.Y. 10033	(212) 960-5211
York College	Jamaica, N.Y. 11451	(718) 262-5104

NORTH CAROLINA

Bennett College	Greensboro, N.C. 27401	(910) 370-8710
Greensboro College	Greensboro, N.C. 27401	(919) 272-7102
Guilford College	Greensboro, N.C. 27410	(910) 316-2159
Meredith College	Raleigh, N.C. 27607	(919) 829-8311
Methodist College	Fayetteville, N.C. 28311	(910) 630-7182
North Carolina		
Wesleyan College	Rocky Mount, N.C. 27804	(919) 985-5214

OHIO

Baldwin-Wallace College	Berea, Ohio 44017	(216) 826-2183
Bluffton College	Bluffton, Ohio 45817	(419) 358-3226
Capital University	Columbus, Ohio 43209	(614) 236-6911
Case West. Reserve U.	Cleveland, Ohio 44106	(216) 368-2866
Defiance College	Defiance, Ohio 43512	(419) 784-4010
Denison University	Granville, Ohio 43023	(614) 587-6428
Heidelberg College	Tiffin, Ohio 44883	(330) 569-5345
Hiram College	Hiram, Ohio 44234	(216) 569-5352
John Carroll University	Univ. Heights, Ohio 44118	(216) 397-4497
Kenyon College	Gambier, Ohio 43022	(330) 427-5256
Marietta College	Marietta, Ohio 45750	(614) 374-4667
Mount Union College	Alliance, Ohio 44601	(216) 823-4880
Muskingum College	New Concord, Ohio 43762	(614) 826-8320
Oberlin College	Oberlin, Ohio 44074	(216) 775-8502
Ohio Northern Univ.	Ada, Ohio 45810	(419) 772-2450
Ohio Wesleyan Univ.	Delaware, Ohio 43015	(614) 368-3727
Otterbein College	Westerville, Ohio 43081	(614) 823-1653
Wilmington College	Wilmington, Ohio 45177	(513) 382-6661
Wittenberg University	Springfield, Ohio 45504	(513) 327-6472
Wooster, College of	Wooster, Ohio 44691	(216) 263-2189

PENNSYLVANIA

Albright College	Reading, Pa. 19612	(610) 921-7535
Allegheny College	Meadville, Pa. 16335	(814) 332-2824
Allentown Col\		
St. Francis de Sales	Center Valley, Pa. 18034	(610) 282-1335
Alvernia College	Reading, Pa. 19607	(610) 796-8261
Beaver College	Glenside, Pa. 19038	(215) 572-2194
Bryn Mawr College	Bryn Mawr, Pa. 19010	(610) 526-5364
Cabrini College	Radnor, Pa. 19087	(610) 902-8386
Carnegie Mellon Univ.	Pittsburgh, Pa. 15213	(412) 268-8555

Cedar Crest College	Allentown, Pa. 18104	(610) 606-4634	
Chestnut Hill College	Philadelphia, Pa. 19118	(215) 248-7060	
College Misericordia	Dallas, Pa. 18612	(717) 674-6294	
Delaware Valley College	Doylestown, Pa. 18901	(215)489-2268	
Dickinson College	Carlisle, Pa. 17013	(717) 245-1320	
Eastern College	St. David's, Pa. 19087	(610) 225-5033	
Elizabethtown College	Elizabethtown, Pa. 17022	(717) 361-1137	
Franklin and Marshall Coll.	Lancaster, Pa. 17604	(717) 291-4104	Div. I in wrestling
Gettysburg College	Gettysburg, Pa. 17325	(717) 337-6400	
Grove City College	Grove City, Pa. 16127	(412) 458-2120	
Gwynedd-Mercy College	Gwynedd Valley, Pa. 19347	(215) 641-5574	
Haverford College	Haverford, Pa. 19041	(610) 896-1117	
Immaculata College	Immaculata, Pa. 19345	(215) 647-4400	
Juniata College	Huntingdon, Pa. 16652	(814) 643-4310	
King's College	Wilkes-Barre, Pa. 18711	(717) 826-5855	
Lebanon Valley College	Annville, Pa. 17003	(717) 867-6261	
Lincoln University	Lincoln Univ., Pa. 19352	(610) 932-8300	
Lycoming College	Williamsport, Pa. 17701	(717) 321-4260	
Marywood College	Scranton, Pa. 18509	(717)961-4724	
Messiah College	Grantham, Pa. 17027	(717) 691-6018	
Moravian College	Bethlehem, Pa. 18018	(610) 861-1534	
Muhlenberg College	Allentown, Pa. 18104	(610) 821-3380	
Neumann College	Aston, Pa. 19014	(610) 558-5627	
Penn State-Behrend Coll.	Erie, Pa. 16563	(814) 898-6379	
Rosemont College	Rosemont, Pa. 19010	(610) 527-0200	
Susquehanna University	Selinsgrove, Pa. 17870	(717) 372-4272	
Swarthmore College	Swarthmore, Pa. 19081	(610) 328-8222	
Thiel College	Greenville, Pa. 16125	(412) 589-2142	
University of Scranton	Scranton, Pa. 18510	(717) 941-7440	
Ursinus College	Collegeville, Pa. 19426	(610) 409-3606	Div. I in field hockey
Washington and Jefferson College	Washington, Pa. 15301	(412) 223-6054	
Waynesburg College	Waynesburg, Pa. 15370	(412) 852-3246	
Widener University	Chester, Pa. 19013	(610) 499-4443	
Wilkes University	Wilkes-Barre, Pa. 18766	(717) 831-4024	Div. I in wrestling
York College	York, Pa. 17405	(717) 846-7788	

PUERTO RICO

American Univ. of Puerto Rico	Bayamon, P.R. 00960	(809) 798-2040

RHODE ISLAND

Rhode Island College	Providence, R.I. 02908	(401) 456-8007
Roger Williams College	Bristol, R.I. 02809	(401) 254-3129
Salve Regina College	Newport, R.I. 02840	(401) 847-6650

TENNESSEE

Fisk University	Nashville, Tenn. 37208	(615) 329-8782
Maryville College	Maryville, Tenn. 37804	(423) 981-8287
Rhodes College	Memphis, Tenn. 38112	(901) 726-3939
University of the South	Sewanee, Tenn. 37383	(615) 598-1388

TEXAS

Hardin-Simmons Univ.	Abilene, Texas 79698	(915) 670-1435
Howard Payne University	Brownwood, Texas 76801	(915) 649-8813
SW University (Texas)	Georgetown, Texas 78626	(512) 863-1618
Trinity University	San Antonio, Texas 78212	(210) 736-8272

VERMONT

Castleton State College	Castleton, Vt. 05735	(802) 468-5611
Johnson State College	Johnson, Vt. 05656	(802) 635-1485
Middlebury College	Middlebury, Vt. 05753	(802) 388-3711
Norwich University	Northfield, Vt. 05663	(802) 485-2232

VIRGINIA

Averett College	Danville, Va. 24541	(804) 791-5701
Bridgewater College	Bridgewater, Va. 22812	(540) 828-2501
Christopher Newport Coll.	Newport News, Va. 23606	(757) 594-7217
Eastern Mennonite Coll.	Harrisonburg, Va. 22801	(540) 432-4439
Emory and Henry College	Emory, Va. 24327	(540) 944-6233
Ferrum College	Ferrum, Va. 24088	(540) 365-4493
Hampden-Sydney Coll.	Hampden-Sydney, Va. 23943	(804) 223-6153
Hollins College	Hollins College, Va. 24020	(540) 362-6435
Lynchburg College	Lynchburg, Va. 24501	(804) 522-8498
Mary Baldwin College	Staunton, Va. 24401	(540) 887-7161
Mary Washington Coll.	Fredericksburg, Va. 22401	(540) 654-1876
Marymount College	Arlington, Va. 22207	(703) 284-1619
Randolph-Macon Coll.	Ashland, Va. 23005	(804) 752-7299
Randolph-Macon Woman's College	Lynchburg, Va. 24503	(804) 947-8536
Roanoke College	Salem, Va. 24153	(540) 375-2337
Shenandoah University	Winchester, Va. 22601	(540) 665-4566
Sweet Briar College	Sweet Briar, Va. 24595	(804) 381-6336
Virginia Wesleyan Coll.	Norfolk, Va. 23502	(757) 455-3302
Washington and Lee Univ.	Lexington, Va. 24450	(540) 463-8671

WEST VIRGINIA

Bethany College	Bethany, W. Va. 26032	(304) 829-7251

WISCONSIN

Beloit College	Beloit, Wis. 53511	(608) 363-2234
Carroll College	Waukesha, Wis. 53186	(414) 524-7320
Carthage College	Kenosha, Wis. 53140	(414) 551-5931
Edgewood College	Madison, Wis. 53711	(608) 257-4861
Lakeland College	Sheboygan, Wis. 53082	(414) 565-1240
Lawrence University	Appleton, Wis. 54912	(414) 832-6513
Milwaukee School of Engineering	Milwaukee, Wis. 53202	(414) 277-7230
Northwestern College	Watertown, Wis. 53094	(414) 262-8117
Ripon College	Ripon, Wis. 54971	(414) 748-8774
St. Norbert College	De Pere, Wis. 54115	(414) 337-3030

University of Wisconsin	Eau Claire, Wis. 54702	(715) 836-3159
University of Wisconsin	La Crosse, Wis. 54601	(608) 785-8616
University of Wisconsin	Oshkosh, Wis. 54901	(414) 424-1034
University of Wisconsin	Platteville, Wis. 53818	(608) 342-1567
University of Wisconsin	River Falls, Wis. 54022	(715) 425-3257
University of Wisconsin	Stevens Point, Wis. 54481	(715) 346-3888
Univ. of Wisconsin, Stout	Menomonie, Wis. 54751	(715) 232-2161
University of Wisconsin	Superior, Wis. 54880	(715) 394-8291
University of Wisconsin	Whitewater, Wis. 53190	(414) 472-4661

NAIA

The National Association of Intercollegiate Athletics includes more than 350 four-year colleges and universities. There is no limit on the number of athletic scholarships, but many are small schools with budget limitations. The country is divided into districts, with playoffs leading to national championships in 11 men's sports and nine women's sports. Conferences can choose to compete in football and basketball at either the Division I or Division II level. In other sports, all NAIA schools compete for the same championships.

CANADA

Simon Fraser University	Burnaby, BC, Can V5A 1S6	(604) 291-3313

ALABAMA

Athens State College	Athens, Ala. 35611	(205) 233-8279
Auburn U. at Montgomery	Montgomery, Ala. 36117	(205) 244-3541
Birmingham-Southern Coll.	Birmingham, Ala. 35254	(205) 226-4936
Faulkner University	Montgomery, Ala. 36109	(334) 260-6159
Huntingdon College	Montgomery, Ala. 36106	(334) 833-4565
Spring Hill College	Mobile, Ala. 36608	(334) 380-3486
Talladega College	Talladega, Ala. 35160	(205) 761-6239
University of Mobile	Mobile, Ala. 36663	(334) 672-5990
University of Montevallo	Montevallo, Ala 35115	(205) 665-6694

ARIZONA

Embry-Riddle Aeronautical Univ.	Prescott, Ariz. 86301	(520) 776-3791

ARKANSAS

Arkansas Tech University	Russellville, Ark. 72801	(501) 968-0345
Harding University	Searcy, Ark. 72149	(501) 279-4305
John Brown University	Siloam Springs, Ark. 72761	(501) 524-7305
Lyon College	Batesville, Ark. 72503	(501) 698-4221
Ouchita Baptist University	Arkadelphia, Ark. 71998	(501) 245-5181
Univ. of Ark. at Pine Bluff	Pine Bluff, Ark. 71611	(501) 543-8675
University of the Ozarks	Clarksville, Ark. 72830	(501) 979-1325
Williams Baptist College	College City, Ark. 72476	(501) 886-6741

CALIFORNIA

Azusa Pacific University	Azusa, Calif. 91702	(818) 812-3024
Bethany College	Scotts Valley, Calif. 95060	(408) 438-3800
Biola University	La Mirada, Calif. 90639	(310) 903-4725
California Baptist College	Riverside, Calif. 92504	(909) 343-4381
California Maritime Acad.	Vallejo, Calif. 94590	(707) 648-4261
Calif. State U. - Monterey Bay	Seaside, Calif. 93955	(408) 582-3715

Christian Heritage Coll.	El Cajon, Calif. 92019	(619) 441-2200
Concordia University	Irvine, Calif. 92612	(714) 854-8002
Dominican College	San Raphael, Calif. 94901	(415) 485-3230
Fresno Pacific College	Fresno, Calif. 93702	(209) 453-2122
Holy Names College	Oakland, Calif. 94619	(510) 436-1491
La Sierra University	Riverside, Calif. 92515	(909) 785-2295
Pacific Christian College	Fullerton, Calif. 92831	(714) 879-3901
Pacific Union College	Angwin, Calif. 94508	(707) 965-6344
Patten College	Oakland, Calif. 94601	(510) 533-8300
Simpson College	Redding, Calif. 96003	(916) 224-8600
The Master's College	Newhall, Calif. 91321	(805) 259-3540
Pt. Loma Nazarene Coll.	San Diego, Calif. 92106	(619) 549-2266
Southern California Coll.	Costa Mesa, Calif. 92626	(714) 556-3610
U.S. International Univ.	San Diego, Calif. 92131	(619) 635-4630
Westmont College	Santa Barbara, Calif. 93108	(805) 565-6010

CONNECTICUT

Teikyo Post University	Waterbury, Conn. 06723	(203) 596-4531

DELAWARE

Goldey-Beacom College	Wilmington, Del. 19808	(302) 998-8814
Wilmington College	New Castle, Del. 19720	(302) 328-9435

FLORIDA

Edward Waters College	Jacksonville, Fla. 32209	(904) 366-2798
Embry-Riddle Aeronautical Univ.	Daytona Beach, Fla. 32114	(904) 226-6526
Flagler College	St. Augustine, Fla. 32085	(904) 829-6481
Florida Memorial College	Miami, Fla. 33054	(305) 626-3690
Northwood University	W. Palm Beach, Fla. 33409	(407) 478-5552
Nova Southeastern Univ.	Fort Lauderdale, Fla. 33314	(305) 475-7345
Palm Beach Atlantic Coll.	W. Palm Beach, Fla. 33416	(561) 803-2527
Saint Thomas University	Miami, Fla. 33054	(305) 628-6678
Warner Southern College	Lake Wales, Fla. 33853	(941) 638-1464
Webber College	Babson Park, Fla. 33827	(941) 638-2953

GEORGIA

Berry College	Mount Berry, Ga. 30149	(706) 236-1743
Brenau College	Gainesville, Ga. 30501	(770) 534-6230
Brewton Parker College	Mount Vernon, Ga. 30445	(912) 583-3206
Clayton State College	Morrow, Ga. 30260	(770) 961-3450
Covenant College	Lookout Mntn., Ga. 30750	(706) 820-1560
Emmanuel College	Franklin Springs, Ga. 30639	(706) 245-7226
Georgia SW College	Americus, Ga. 31709	(912) 931-2222
LaGrange College	LaGrange, Ga. 30240	(706) 812-7262
Life College	Marietta, Ga. 30060	(770) 424-0554
North Georgia College	Dahlonega, Ga. 30597	(706) 864-1627
Piedmont College	Demorest, Ga. 30535	(706) 778-3000
Shorter College	Rome, Ga. 30165	(706) 233-7347
So. Polytechnic State Univ.	Marietta, Ga. 30060	(404) 528-7350

Thomas College   Thomasville, Ga. 31792   (912) 226-1621

HAWAII

Brigham Young
  Univ./Hawaii   Laie, Hawaii 96762   (808) 293-3760
Hawaii Pacific University Honolulu, Hawaii 96813   (808) 544-0220

IDAHO

Albertson College of Idaho Caldwell, Idaho 83605   (208) 459-5850
Lewis Clark State College   Lewiston, Idaho 83501   (208) 799-2275
Northwest Nazarene Coll.   Nampa, Idaho 83686   (208) 467-8348

ILLINOIS

Barat College   Lake Forest, Ill. 60045   (847) 615-5664
Illinois Institute of Tech. Chicago, Ill. 60616   (312) 567-3298
Judson College   Elgin, Ill. 60123   (847) 695-2500
McKendree College   Lebanon, Ill. 62254   (618) 537-6871
Olivet Nazarene Univ.   Kankakee, Ill. 60901   (815) 939-5123
Robert Morris College   Chicago, Ill. 60601   (312) 836-4627
Rosary College   River Forest, Ill. 60305   (312) 366-2490
College of Saint Francis Joliet, Ill. 60435   (815) 740-3464
Saint Xavier College   Chicago, Ill. 60655   (312) 298-3100
Trinity Christian College Palos Heights, Ill. 60463   (708) 597-3000
Trinity International Univ. Deerfield, Ill. 60015   (708) 317-7091
Univ. of Ill. at Springfield Springfield, Ill. 62794   (217) 786-6674

INDIANA

Bethel College   Mishawaka, Ind. 46545   (219) 257-3345
Goshen College   Goshen, Ind. 46526   (219) 535-7492
Grace College   Winona Lake, Ind. 46590   (219) 372-5224
Huntingdon College   Huntingdon, Ind. 46750   (219) 356-6000
Indiana Institute of Tech. Fort Wayne, Ind. 46803   (219) 422-5561
Indiana Univ. Southeast   New Albany, Ind. 47150   (812) 941-2432
Indiana U. at South Bend South Bend, Ind. 46634   (219) 288-6058
Indiana Wesleyan Univ.   Marion, Ind. 46953   (317) 677-2317
Marian College   Indianapolis, Ind. 46222   (317) 929-0370
Purdue Univ. Calumet   Hammond, Ind. 46323   (219) 989-2540
Saint Francis College   Fort Wayne, Ind. 46808   (219) 434-3243
Taylor University   Upland, Ind. 46989   (317) 998-5341
Tri-State University   Angola, Ind. 46703   (219) 665-4143

IOWA

Briar Cliff College   Sioux City, Iowa 51104   (712) 279-1706
Clarke College   Dubuque, Iowa 52001   (319) 588-6462
Dordt College   Sioux Center, Iowa 51250   (712) 722-6305
Graceland College   Lamoni, Iowa 50140   (515) 784-5106
Grand View College   Des Moines, Iowa 50316   (515) 263-2897
Iowa Wesleyan College   Mount Pleasant, Iowa 52641 (319) 385-6301
Marycrest University   Davenport, Iowa 52804   (319) 326-9596

Mount Mercy College	Cedar Rapids, Iowa 52402	(319) 363-8213
Mount Saint Clare College	Clinton, Iowa 52732	(319) 242-4023
Northwestern College	Orange City, Iowa 51041	(712) 737-7280
Saint Ambrose University	Davenport, Iowa 52803	(319) 333-6233
Westmar University	Le Mars, Iowa 51031	(712) 546-2575

KANSAS

Baker University	Baldwin City, Kan. 66006	(913) 594-6451
Benedictine College	Atchison, Kan. 66002	(913) 367-5340
Bethany College	Lindsborg, Kan. 67456	(913) 227-3380
Bethel College	North Newton, Kan. 67117	(316) 283-2500
Friends University	Wichita, Kan. 67213	(316) 268-7627
Kansas Newman College	Wichita, Kan. 67213	(316) 942-4291
Kansas Wesleyan Univ.	Salina, Kan. 67401	(913) 827-5541
McPherson College	McPherson, Kan. 67460	(316) 241-0731
MidAmerica Nazarene Coll.	Olathe, Kan. 66062	(913) 782-3750
Ottawa University	Ottawa, Kan. 66067	(913) 242-5200
Saint Mary College	Leavenworth, Kan. 66048	(913) 682-5151
Southwestern College	Winfield, Kan. 67156	(316) 221-8327
Sterling College	Sterling, Kan. 67579	(316) 278-4285
Tabor College	Hillsboro, Kan. 67063	(316) 947-3121

KENTUCKY

Alice Lloyd College	Pippa Passes, Ky. 41844	(606) 368-2101
Asbury College	Wilmore, Ky. 40390	(606) 858-3511
Berea College	Berea, Ky. 40404	(606) 986-9341
Brescia College	Owensboro, Ky. 42301	(502) 686-4317
Campbellsville College	Campbellsville, Ky. 42718	(502) 789-5009
Cumberland College	Williamsburg, Ky. 40769	(606) 549-4839
Georgetown College	Georgetown, Ky. 40324	(502) 863-8007
Lindsey Wilson College	Columbia, Ky. 42728	(502) 384-2126
Midway College	Midway, Ky. 40347	(606) 846-5387
Pikeville College	Pikeville, Ky. 41501	(606) 432-9313
Spalding University	Louisville, Ky. 40203	(502) 588-7174
Sue Bennett College	London, Ky. 40741	(606) 864-2238
Transylvania University	Lexington, Ky. 40508	(606) 233-8270
Union College	Barbourville, Ky. 40906	(606) 546-1233

LOUISIANA

Dillard University	New Orleans, La. 70122	(504) 286-4644
Louisiana College	Pineville, La. 71359	(318) 487-7131
Louisiana State Univ., Shreveport	Shreveport, La. 71115	(318) 797-5194
Loyola University	New Orleans, La. 70118	(504) 865-3137
Southern Univ. at New Orleans	New Orleans, La. 70126	(504) 286-5195
Xavier U. of Louisiana	New Orleans, La. 70125	(504) 486-7411

MAINE

Husson College	Bangor, Maine 04401	(207) 947-7029
Saint Joseph's College	Standish, Maine 04084	(207) 893-6670

Thomas College	Waterville, Maine 04901	(207) 873-0771
U. of Maine at Farmington	Farmington, Maine 04938	(207) 778-7142
U. of Maine at Machias	Machias, Maine 04654	(207) 255-1290
U. of Maine at Presque Isle	Presque Isle, Maine 04769	(207) 768-9477
University of New England	Biddeford, Maine 04005	(207) 283-0171

MARYLAND

Columbia Union College	Takoma Park, Md. 20912	(301) 891-4024

MASSACHUSETTS

Atlantic Union College	S. Lancaster, Mass. 01561	(508) 368-2142

MICHIGAN

Aquinas College	Grand Rapids, Mich. 49506	(616) 459-8281
Concordia College	Ann Arbor, Mich. 48105	(313) 995-7343
Cornerstone College	Grand Rapids, Mich. 49505	(616) 285-9425
Hillsdale College	Hillsdale, Mich. 49242	(517) 437-7364
Madonna University	Livonia, Mich. 48150	(313)432-5610
Siena Heights College	Adrian, Mich. 49221	(517) 263-0731
Spring Arbor College	Spring Arbor, Mich. 49283	(517) 750-6503
U. of Michigan-Dearborn	Dearborn, Mich. 48128	(313) 593-5540

MINNESOTA

Concordia Coll.-St. Paul	St. Paul, Minn. 55104	(612) 641-8485
C. of Saint Scholastica	Duluth, Minn. 55811	(218) 723-6199
Northwestern College	Saint Paul, Minn. 55113	(612) 631-5238
U. of Minnesota-Crookston	Crookston, Minn. 56716	(218) 281-8415

MISSISSIPPI

Belhaven College	Jackson, Miss. 39202	(601) 968-5956
Blue Mountain College	Blue Mountain, Miss. 38610	(601) 685-4771
Tougaloo College	Tougaloo, Miss. 39174	(601) 977-7809
William Carey College	Hattiesburg, Miss. 39401	(601) 582-6415

MISSOURI

Avila College	Kansas City, Mo. 64145	(816) 942-8400
Central Methodist College	Fayette, Mo. 65248	(816) 248-3392
College of the Ozarks	Point Lookout, Mo. 65726	(417) 334-6411
Columbia College	Columbia, Mo. 65216	(314) 875-7410
Culver-Stockton College	Canton, Mo. 63435	(217) 231-6393
Evangel College	Springfield, Mo. 65802	(417) 865-2815
Hannibal-LaGrange Coll.	Hannibal, Mo. 63401	(573) 221-3675
Harris Stowe State Coll.	St. Louis, Mo. 63103	(314) 340-3530
Lindenwood College	St. Charles, Mo. 63301	(314) 949-4880
Missouri Baptist College	St. Louis, Mo. 63141	(314) 434-1115
Missouri Valley College	Marshall, Mo. 65340	(816) 831-4168
Park College	Parkville, Mo. 64152	(816) 741-2000
Rockhurst College	Kansas City, Mo. 64110	(816) 501-4141
St. Louis College of Pharmacy	St. Louis, Mo. 63110	(314) 367-8700

William Jewell College	Liberty, Mo. 64068	(816) 781-7700
William Woods College	Fulton, Mo. 65251	(314) 592-4387

MONTANA

Carroll College	Helena, Mont. 59625	(406) 447-4481
Montana State University-Northern	Havre, Mont. 59501	(406) 265-3761
Montana Tech of the Univ. of Montana	Butte, Mont. 59701	(406) 496-4292
Rocky Mountain College	Billings, Mont. 59102	(406) 657-1124
Western Montana College	Dillon, Mont. 59725	(406) 683-7220

NEBRASKA

Bellevue College	Bellevue, Neb. 68005	(402) 293-3784
Concordia College	Seward, Neb. 68434	(402) 643-7328
Dana College	Blair, Neb. 68008	(402) 426-7296
Doane College	Crete, Neb. 68333	(402) 826-8281
Hastings College	Hastings, Neb. 68901	(402) 461-7331
Midland Lutheran College	Fremont, Neb. 68025	(402) 721-5480
Nebraska Wesleyan Univ.	Lincoln, Neb. 68504	(402) 465-2360
Peru State College	Peru, Neb. 68421	(402) 872-2207
College of Saint Mary	Omaha, Neb. 68124	(402) 399-2359
York College	York, Neb. 68467	(402) 363-5742

NEW HAMPSHIRE

Notre Dame College	Manchester, N.H. 03104	(603) 669-4298

NEW JERSEY

Bloomfield College	Bloomfield, N.J. 07003	(201) 748-9000
Caldwell College	Caldwell, N.J. 07006	(201) 228-4424
Felician College	Lodi, N.J. 07644	(201) 778-1190
Georgian Court College	Lakewood, N.J. 08701	(908) 363-2374

NEW MEXICO

College of the Southwest	Hobbs, N.M. 88240	(505) 392-6561

NEW YORK

Daemen College	Amherst, N.Y. 14226	(716) 839-8346
Dominican College	Orangeburg, N.Y. 10962	(914) 359-7800
Houghton College	Houghton, N.Y. 14744	(716) 567-9364
Nyack College	Nyack, N.Y. 10960	(914) 358-1710
Roberts Wesleyan Coll.	Rochester, N.Y. 14624	(716) 594-6512
St. Thomas Aquinas Coll.	Sparkill, N.Y. 10976	(914) 398-4058

NORTH CAROLINA

Barber-Scotia College	Concord, N.C. 28025	(704) 793-4954
Montreat-Anderson Coll.	Montreat, N.C. 28757	(704) 669-3011

NORTH DAKOTA

Dickinson State Univ.	Dickinson, N.D. 58601	(701) 227-2159
Jamestown College	Jamestown, N.D. 58405	(701) 252-3467
Mayville State University	Mayville, N.D. 58257	(701) 786-4658
Minot State University	Minot, N.D. 58702	(701) 857-3042
University of Mary	Bismarck, N.D. 58504	(701) 255-7500
Valley City State Univ.	Valley City, N.D. 58072	(701) 845-7211

OHIO

Cedarville College	Cedarville, Ohio 45314-0601	(513) 766-7755
Central State University	Wilberforce, Ohio 45384	(513) 376-6345
Malone College	Canton, Ohio 44709	(216) 471-8296
Coll. of Mount St. Joseph	Cincinnati, Ohio 45233	(513) 244-4311
Mt. Vernon Nazarene Coll.	Mount Vernon, Ohio 43050	(614) 397-1244
Notre Dame Coll. of Ohio	Cleveland, Ohio 44121	(216) 381-1680
Ohio Dominican College	Columbus, Ohio 43219	(614) 251-4535
Shawnee State Univ.	Portsmouth, Ohio 45662	(614) 355-2263
Tiffin University	Tiffin, Ohio 44883	(419) 448-3452
University of Findlay	Findlay, Ohio 45840	(419) 424-4651
University of Rio Grande	Rio Grande, Ohio 45674	(614) 245-5353
Urbana University	Urbana, Ohio 43078	(513) 484-1325
Walsh University	Canton, Ohio 44720	(330) 490-7035
Wilberforce University	Wilberforce, Ohio 45384	(513) 376-2911

OKLAHOMA

Bartlesville Wesleyan Coll.	Bartlesville, Okla. 74006	(918) 333-6259
East Central University	Ada, Okla. 74820	(405) 332-8000
Langston University	Langston, Okla. 73050	(405) 466-3262
Northeastern State Univ.	Tahlequah, Okla. 74464	(918) 456-5511
NW Oklahoma State U.	Alva, Okla. 73717	(405) 327-8626
Oklahoma Baptist Univ.	Shawnee, Okla. 74801	(405) 878-2132
Oklahoma Christian Univ.	Oklahoma City, Okla. 73136	(405) 425-5360
Oklahoma City University	Oklahoma City, Okla. 73106	(405) 521-5302
Okla. Pandhandle State U.	Goodwell, Okla. 73939	(405) 349-2611
Phillips University	Enid, Okla. 73701	(405) 548-2278
SE Oklahoma State U.	Durant, Okla. 74701	(405) 924-0121
Southern Nazarene Univ.	Bethany, Okla. 73008	(405) 491-6339
SW Oklahoma State U.	Weatherford, Okla. 73096	(405) 774-3182
U. of Science & Arts of Oklahoma	Chickasha, Okla. 73018	(405) 224-3140

OREGON

Cascade College	Portland, Ore. 97220	(503) 255-7060
Concordia College	Portland, Ore. 97211	(503) 280-8516
E. Oregon State College	LaGrande, Ore. 97850	(541) 962-3363
George Fox College	Newberg, Ore. 97132	(503) 538-8383
Lewis and Clark College	Portland, Ore. 97219	(503) 768-7548
Linfield College	McMinnville, Ore. 97128	(503) 434-2229
Oregon Institute of Tech.	Klamath Falls, Ore. 97601	(541) 885-1625
Pacific University	Forest Grove, Ore. 97116	(503) 359-2260

South. Oregon State Coll.	Ashland, Ore. 97520	(541) 552-6500
Western Baptist College	Salem, Ore. 97301	(503) 375-7021
W. Oregon State College	Monmouth, Ore. 97361	(503) 838-8252
Willamette University	Salem, Ore. 97301	(503) 370-6217

PENNSYLVANIA

Carlow College	Pittsburgh, Pa. 15213	(412) 578-6345
Geneva College	Beaver Falls, Pa. 15010	(412) 847-6648
Holy Family College	Philadelphia, Pa. 19114	(215) 632-8284
Phil. C. of Pharmacy & Science	Philadelphia, Pa. 19104	(215) 596-8916
Point Park College	Pittsburgh, Pa. 15222	(412) 392-3843
Saint Vincent College	Latrobe, Pa. 15650	(412) 539-9761
Seton Hill College	Greensburg, Pa. 15601	(412) 838-4259
U. of Pittsburgh at Bradford	Bradford, Pa. 16701	(814) 362-7523
Westminster College	New Wilmington, Pa. 16172	(412) 946-7308

SOUTH CAROLINA

Allen University	Columbia, S.C. 29204	(803) 376-5753
Anderson College	Anderson, S.C. 29621	(864) 231-2022
Benedict College	Columbia, S.C. 29204	(803) 253-5275
Claflin College	Orangeburg, S.C. 29115	(803) 534-2710
Coker College	Hartsville, S.C. 29550	(803) 383-8071
Columbia College	Columbia, S.C. 29203	(803) 786-3723
Johnson & Wales Univ.	Charleston, S.C. 29403	(803) 571-3298
Limestone College	Gaffney, S.C. 29340	(803) 488-4561
Morris College	Sumter, S.C. 29150	(803) 775-9371
North Greenville College	Tigerville, S.C. 29688	(864) 977-7151
Southern Wesleyan Coll.	Central, S.C. 29630	(803) 639-2453
Voorhees College	Denmark, S.C. 29042	(803) 793-3351

SOUTH DAKOTA

Black Hills State Univ.	Spearfish, S.D. 57799	(605) 642-6881
Dakota State University	Madison, S.D. 57042	(605) 256-5229
Dakota Wesleyan Univ.	Mitchell, S.D. 57301	(605) 995-2875
Huron University	Huron, S.D. 57350	(605) 352-9465
Mount Marty College	Yankton, S.D. 57078	(605) 668-1529
National College	Rapid City, S.D. 57709	(605) 394-4825
Presentation College	Aberdeen, S.D. 57401	(605) 225-0420
South Dakota Tech	Rapid City, S.D. 57701	(605) 394-2352
University of Sioux Falls	Sioux Falls, S.C. 57105	(605) 331-6656

TENNESSEE

Belmont University	Nashville, Tenn. 37212	(615) 460-5547
Bethel College	McKenzie, Tenn. 38201	(901) 352-1000
Bryan College	Dayton, Tenn. 37321	(615) 775-2041
Christian Brothers Coll.	Memphis, Tenn. 38104	(901) 321-3374
Cumberland University	Lebanon, Tenn. 37087	(615) 444-2562
Freed-Hardeman College	Henderson, Tenn. 38340	(901) 989-6901
King College	Bristol, Tenn. 37620	(615) 652-4849

Lambuth Univesity	Jackson, Tenn. 38301	(901) 425-3398
Lee College	Cleveland, Tenn. 37311	(423) 614-8440
Lipscomb University	Nashville, Tenn. 37204	(615) 269-1795
Martin Methodist College	Pulaski, Tenn. 38478	(615) 363-9872
Milligan College	Milligan Coll., Tenn. 37682	(423) 461-8990
Tenn. Wesleyan College	Athens, Tenn. 37371	(423) 745-7504
Trevecca Nazarene Coll.	Nashville, Tenn. 37210	(615) 248-1200
Tusculum College	Greeneville, Tenn. 37743	(423) 636-7323
Union University	Jackson, Tenn. 38305	(901) 661-5277

TEXAS

Ambassador College	Big Sandy, Texas 75755	(903) 636-2090
Austin College	Sherman, Texas 75091	(903) 813-2499
Concordia University	Austin, Texas 78705	(512) 452-7661
Dallas Baptist University	Dallas, Texas 75211	(214) 333-5340
East Texas Baptist Univ.	Marshall, Texas 75670	(903) 935-7963
Hardin-Simmons Univ.	Abilene, Texas 79698	(915) 670-1473
Houston Baptist Univ.	Houston, Texas 77074	(713) 995-3205
Howard Payne University	Brownwood, Texas 76801	(915)649-8011
Huston-Tillotson College	Austin, Texas 78702	(512) 505-3050
Incarnate Word University	San Antonio, Texas 78209	(210) 829-6053
Jarvis Christian College	Hawkins, Texas 75765	(903) 769-5763
LeTourneau University	Longview, Texas 75607	(903) 233-3371
Lubbock Christian Univ.	Lubbock, Texas 79407	(806) 796-8800
McMurry College	Abilene, Texas 79697	(915) 691-6276
Midwestern State Univ.	Wichita Falls, Texas 76308	(817) 689-4774
Northwood University	Cedar Hill, Texas 75104	(214) 293-5439
Prairie View A&M Univ.	Prairie View, Texas 77446	(409) 857-4398
Saint Edward's University	Austin, Texas 78704	(512) 448-8450
Saint Mary's University	San Antonio, Texas 78228	(210) 436-3528
Schreiner College	Kerrville, Texas 78028	(210) 896-5411
SW Adventist College	Keene, Texas 76059	(817) 645-3921
Sul Ross State University	Alpine, Texas 79832	(915) 837-8226
Texas Lutheran College	Seguin, Texas 78155	(210) 372-8122
Texas Wesleyan Univ.	Fort Worth, Texas 76105	(817) 531-4948
U. of Mary Hardin-Baylor	Belton, Texas 76513	(817) 939-4618
U. of Texas at Dallas	Richardson, Texas 75083	(214) 883-2094
U. of Texas at the Permian Basin	Odessa, Texas 79762	(915) 552-2675
Univ. of Texas at Tyler	Tyler, Texas75799	(903) 566-7024
Wayland Baptist Univ.	Plainview, Texas 79072	(806) 296-4739
Wiley College	Marshall, Texas 75670	(903) 927-3350

UTAH

Westminster College	Salt Lake City, Utah 84105	(801) 488-4211

VERMONT

Castleton State College	Castleton, Vt. 05735	(802) 468-5611
Green Mountain College	Poultney, Vt. 05674	(802) 287-8238
Johnson State College	Johnson, Vt. 05656	(802) 635-1285

Lyndon State College	Lyndonville, Vt. 05851	(802) 626-6477
Coll. of St. Joseph in Vermont	Rutland, Vt. 05701	(802) 773-5900

VIRGINIA

Bluefield College	Bluefield, Va. 24605	(540) 326-4349
Clinch Valley College	Wise, Va. 24293	(540) 328-0259
Virginia Intermont College	Bristol, Va. 24201	(703) 669-6101

WASHINGTON

Central Washington Univ.	Ellensburg, Wash. 98926	(509) 963-1914
Evergreen State College	Olympia, Wash. 98505	(360) 866-6000
Northwest College	Kirkland, Wash. 98083	(206) 889-2754
Pacific Lutheran University	Tacoma, Wash. 98447	(206) 535-7361
Saint Martin's College	Lacey, Wash. 98503	(360) 438-4372
Seattle University	Seattle, Wash. 98122	(206) 296-6400
University of Puget Sound	Tacoma, Wash. 98416	(206) 756-3426
Western Washington Univ.	Bellingham, Wash. 98225	(360) 676-3109
Whitman College	Walla Walla, Wash. 99362	(509) 527-5288
Whitworth College	Spokane, Wash. 99251	(509) 466-1000

WEST VIRGINIA

The Coll. of West Virginia	Beckley, W. Va. 25802	(304) 253-7351
Ohio Valley College	Parkersburg, W. Va. 26101	(304) 485-7384
W. Virginia State Coll.	Institute, W.Va. 25112	(304) 766-3165

WISCONSIN

Cardinal Stritch College	Milwaukee, Wis. 53217	(414) 352-5400
Concordia University	Mequon, Wis. 53092	(414) 243-4255
Marian C. of Fond du Lac	Fond du Lac, Wis. 54935	(414) 923-7625
Mount Senario	Ladysmith, Wis. 54848	(715) 532-5511
Northland College	Ashland, Wis. 54806	(715) 682-1245
Viterbo College	LaCrosse, Wis. 54601	(608) 796-3811
Wisconsin Lutheran Coll.	Milwaukee, Wis. 53226	(414) 443-8853

Appendix A:
Sample Sports Resume

D r. Jeff Irving, an executive search consultant who works with professional resumes all the time, developed a sports resume using the same techniques. Study this model and note his suggestions:

- Put your name and social security number on every page.
- Be as concise as possible. Never use more than three well-spaced pages.
- Give a brief description of your high school.
- Put your academic credentials first, listing current courses, grade point average, test scores and any academic honors (always update this).
- List your sports experience, highlighting only the important things, including any national or regional honors and any meets, teams, camps, etc. outside school. Give all coaches' names, addresses and phone numbers. List your personal statistics and records, depending on your particular sport. For example, the model resume is for a rower, so the ergometer statistic is vitally important. Use reverse chronology, giving the most recent experience first, and limit the list to the last two years (keep this up to date as well).
- List other activities and interests, including any community work you may have done.
- Use good bright white stationery. Irving suggests 24-pound basis-weight paper with a 25 percent cotton content. This is not expensive or hard to find. Check out your local discount office supply store. Don't ruin your efforts with cheap paper.
- Write a cover letter, simply stating, for example, "I am a junior and member of the tennis team at W. R. Brown High School here in Anytown. I am very interested in learning more about Wossamatta U. and would appreciate any information you could send me. . . ."
- *NOTE:* Do a first draft of your resume. Then set it aside for a week. Have you done a good job of highlighting your sports career? Does it really matter that you won the Fun Fair Derby in the fourth grade? Note in the model that Jonathan Doe lists only his rowing experience, although he is also a swimmer. Rowing is the sport he wants to take to college, so he concentrates on that. By simply listing swimming, he lets coaches know he has some versatility.

When you have this resume together, keep it up to date and have copies with you on campus visits and for any communications with college personnel. You will want to give copies to your guidance counselors and coaches. Don't hesitate to ask for their help in drafting the resume, but take the responsibility to make a start. Don't expect them to do it for you.

Sample Sports Resume

RESUME

Johnathan Henry Doe

SSN: 000-00-0000
345 Maple Drive
Anytown, USA 10000
(010) 123-4567

Date of Graduation   June, 1998

Secondary Education

Presently enrolled at W.R. Brown High School in Anytown, USA. W.R. Brown has a student body of approximately 1900 in grades 10 through 12.

Grades and Tests

Present GPA: 3.5 of 4.0
Preliminary SAT: Verbal–90th percentile
                    Mathematics–74th percentile
                    (sophomore year results)

Junior Year Subjects

Advanced Placement Biology   French IV
American Civilization,   Trigonometry/Elementary functions
   honors English/History   Engineering Drawing

Sports

Crew: 8, 9, 10
Swimming: 9, 10

Recent Rowing Experience

Summer 1996:   Attended the Junior Men's Eastern Sculling Camp.
                (First experience with sculling.)

                Anytown State Rowing Championships
                Men's Junior Double – Bronze medal
                (Rowed stroke, first sculling competition and
                   first at 2000 meters.)

        Coach: Mr. Irv Brown
                Tagmont Rowing Club
                Home: (010) 789-1011

Johnathan Henry Doe, page 2
SSN: 000-00-0000

Spring 1996:   Rowed 4 seat on the W. R. Brown Varsity Heavyweight Eight.
(Only sophomore to make the boat.)

Regional Scholastic Rowing Association Championship Regatta. Varsity Heavyweight Eight – Gold Medal.

Loving Cup Regatta.
Varsity Heavyweight Eight – Bronze Medal.

Anytown Rowing Association Nationals.
Varsity Heavyweight Eight – Fourth Place.

Coach: Mr. C. Patrick Cooper
Head Coach
W. R. Brown High School
Office: (010) 121-3141
Home: (010) 516-1718

Fall 1995:   Rowed stroke in a Four with Coxswain made up of
W.R. Brown rowers.

John Carlyle Memorial Regatta.
High School Four with Coxswain – Silver Medal.

Head of the Hunting Pond Regatta.
Championship Four with Coxswain – Fourth place.

Coach: Mr. Bob Young
Waterlovers Rowing Club
Home: (010) 192-0212
Office: (010) 223-2425

Personal Data

Date of Birth: November 22, 1979

Present Height: 6'3"
Present Weight: 183 lbs.

2500 meter ergometer test: 8.33, taken in April, 1996.
75 lbs. bench pull/five minutes: 155 repetitions, taken in April, 1996.

–Format courtesy Jeffrey Irving Associates, Inc.

Appendix B
College Checklist

Coach Randy Lambert, athletic director and men's basketball coach at Maryville College, devised this checklist for high school coaches to use to keep track of their seniors. Individual student-athletes can easily use it, too. Unfortunately, it's not that hard to let something slip by undone. Individuals using this checklist may want to add lines for "sports resume sent" and "video sent," whenever applicable.

STEPS INVOLVED	PROSPECTIVE COLLEGES			
	A. _____	B. _____	C. _____	D. _____
I. Admission Process				
A. Application for admission completed	_____	_____	_____	_____
B. High School transcript sent	_____	_____	_____	_____
C. National test scores sent	_____	_____	_____	_____
D. Campus visit made	_____	_____	_____	_____
E. Interviewed by college coach	_____	_____	_____	_____
II. Financial Aid Process				
A. Financial aid form sent for analysis	_____	_____	_____	_____
B. Results sent to college financial aid office	_____	_____	_____	_____
C. Financial aid package designed	_____	_____	_____	_____
D. Package accepted	_____	_____	_____	_____
E. Deposit for final commitment	_____	_____	_____	_____

Courtesy Coach Randy Lambert, Athletic Director, Maryville College

Appendix C

Sample Letters

Sample Letter 1

Jack O. Rollins
2025 Dardon Dr.
Smalltown, Anystate 00009

Coach U. R. Quick
Track and Cross Country Coach
Athletics Department
State University
Statesville, Anystate

Dear Coach Quick:

I will be a senior at Alexander Carlyle High School this fall. I have run track and cross country for the past three years. During my freshman and sophomore years I ran track and cross country, and played soccer at County High School in Wyoming. My coach, Henry Harrison, believes in relatively low-mileage training for high school runners, and I look forward to substantial improvement in my performance throughout college.

I believe I could be a real asset to the athletic program at State University. I would be interested in learning of opportunities for athletic scholarship assistance. I am aware of the tremendous academic and athletic reputation of State U. My parents both graduated from your arch rival, State Tech in 1973; my sister will be a junior at State Tech this fall.

I have enclosed a brief resume outlining my athletic accomplishments. I would appreciate it if you would provide me with information about your track and cross country programs. Thank you very much.

Sincerely,

Jack O. Rollins

Enclosure

Sample Letter 2

Jack O. Rollins
2025 Dardon Dr.
Smalltown , Anystate 00009

Coach U. R. Quick
Track and Cross Country Coach
Athletic Department
State University
Statesville, Anystate

Dear Coach Quick:

Thank you for meeting with me yesterday and going over the academic and athletic programs at State U. My father and I were very impressed with the campus, the athletic facilities and you as a coach. As you requested, I have enclosed a copy of my cross country schedule for this fall. As you can see, there are a few free weekends. I will speak with my coach, Henry Harrison, to see whether I should wait until after the season to make campus visits. I really want to visit State U. during the fall and will stay in touch.

Although you seemed familiar with my background, I have enclosed a brief resume outlining my academic and athletic accomplishments to date.

Thank you again, Coach Quick, for the opportunity to meet with you and see the State U. campus.

Sincerely,

Jack O. Rollins

Enclosure